WHY SHOULD WE READ AND DISCUSS THE BOOKS OF THE BIBLE THAT ARE COLLECTIONS OF SONG LYRICS?

We all know how to say the polite, respectable things about God. But how do we put into words our questions and doubts about God, our frustrations and disappointments with him? Is it proper to give a voice to our darkest spiritual experiences of suffering, depression, and despair? And if, on other occasions, we feel as if we're experiencing a little bit of heaven right here on earth, how can we describe the glories we're tasting? Where do we find the words, when words aren't enough to begin with?

Throughout the ages people have turned to song to express what the spoken word can barely convey. This has always been true of God's people in particular. The songwriters of ancient Israel have left us a rich legacy. They created powerful expressions of the heights and depths of their experiences with God. Over the centuries people used those songs again and again to put their own experiences into words. Eventually many of these songs were gathered into the biblical books of Psalms, Lamentations, and Song of Songs. While their tunes have now been lost, their lyric poetry still speaks eloquently and evocatively today.

In these compositions we encounter an incredibly broad and deep range of spiritual experiences, from people in the depths of despair barely hanging on to their faith to others basking in the glories of heaven on earth. We hear thoughts and feelings expressed that we may have had ourselves, but weren't sure we could or should put into words. If you want to broaden your own spiritual experiences, if you want to know how to speak about them more meaningfully, and if you want to find inspiration in the struggles and triumphs of people of faith who've gone before you, get together with some friends and use this guide to read and discuss the biblical books that are collections of song lyrics: Psalms, Lamentations, and Song of Songs.

UNDERSTANDING THE
BOOKS OF THE BIBLE

PSALMS
LAMENTATIONS
SONG OF SONGS

Also available in the
UNDERSTANDING THE BOOKS OF THE BIBLE series:

John
Genesis
Wisdom: Proverbs/Ecclesiastes/James
Biblical Apocalypses: Daniel/Revelation
Paul's Journey Letters: Thessalonians/Corinthians/
      Galatians/Romans
Luke–Acts
Job—November 2011
Paul's Prison Letters: Colossians/Ephesians/Philemon/
      Philippians/Timothy/Titus—November 2011

Future releases:

Exodus/Leviticus/Numbers
New Covenants: Deuteronomy/Hebrews
Samuel–Kings

Isaiah
Amos/Hosea/Micah/Zephaniah/Nahum/Habakkuk
Jeremiah
Ezekiel
Obadiah/Haggai/Zechariah/Jonah/Joel/Malachi

Chronicles/Ezra/Nehemiah/Esther

Matthew
Mark

Peter/Jude/John

PSALMS
LAMENTATIONS
SONG OF SONGS

Christopher R. Smith

Transforming lives through God's Word

Biblica provides God's Word to people through translation, publishing and Bible engagement in Africa, Asia Pacific, Europe, Latin America, Middle East, and North America. Through its worldwide reach, Biblica engages people with God's Word so that their lives are transformed through a relationship with Jesus Christ.

Biblica Publishing
We welcome your questions and comments.

1820 Jet Stream Drive, Colorado Springs, CO 80921 USA
www.Biblica.com

Understanding the Books of the Bible: Psalms/Lamentations/Song of Songs
ISBN-13: 978-1-60657-061-6

CONTENTS

HOW THESE STUDY GUIDES ARE DIFFERENT

Did you know you could read and study the Bible without using any chapters or verses? The chapter divisions used in most modern Bibles were added more than a thousand years after the biblical books were written. The verse numbers were added more than three centuries after that. If you grew up with the chapter-and-verse system, it may feel like part of the inspired Word of God. But it's not. Those little numbers aren't holy, and when you read and study the Bible without them, you'll hear its message more clearly than ever before.

The books of the Bible are real "books." They're meant to be experienced the same way other books are: as exciting, interesting works that keep you turning pages right to the end and then make you want to go back and savor each part. The UNDERSTANDING THE BOOKS OF THE BIBLE series of study guides will help you do that with the Bible.

While you can use these guides with any version or translation, they're especially designed to be used with *The Books of the Bible*, an edition of the Scriptures from Biblica that takes out the chapter and verse numbers and presents the biblical books in their natural form. Here's what people are saying about reading the Bible this way:

I love it. I find myself understanding Scripture in a new way, with a fresh lens, and I feel spiritually refreshed as a result. I learn much more through stories being told, and with this new format, I feel the truth of the story come alive for me.

Reading Scripture this way flows beautifully. I don't miss the chapter and verse numbers. I like them gone. They got in the way.

I've been a reader of the Bible all of my life. But after reading just a few pages without chapters and verses, I was amazed at what I'd been missing all these years.

For more information about *The Books of the Bible* or to obtain a copy of this specially designed edition, visit http://www.Biblica.com/TheBooks. Watch this site for a four-volume set comprising the entire Bible in this format, coming soon.

For people who are used to chapters and verses, reading and studying the Bible without them may take a little getting used to. It's like when you get a new smart phone or move from using a laptop to a tablet. You have to unlearn some old ways of doing things and learn some new ways. But it's not too long until you catch on to how the new system works and you find you can do a lot of things you couldn't do before.

Here are some of the ways you and your group will have a better experience of the Scriptures by using these study guides.

YOU'LL UNDERSTAND WHOLE BOOKS

Imagine going to a friend's house to watch a movie you've never seen before. After only a couple of scenes, your friend stops the film and says, "So, tell me what you think of it so far." When you give your best shot at a reply, based on the little you've seen, your friend says, "You know, there's a scene in another movie that always makes me think of this one." He switches to a different movie and before you know it, you're watching a scene from the middle of another film.

Who would ever try to watch a movie this way? Yet many study guides take this approach to the Bible. They have you read a few paragraphs from one book, then jump to a passage in another book. The UNDERSTANDING THE

Books of the Bible series doesn't do that. Instead, these study guides focus on understanding the message and meaning of one book at a time. So you won't read a few verses from the Psalms, Song of Songs, or Lamentations and then jump to another place in the Bible. Instead, you'll come to understand each of these books as a whole, so you can then recognize more clearly how what they say relates to other parts of the Bible.

In the case of the book of Psalms, before you try to read through the entire book, it's important to understand each of the individual psalms first, since they're all independent compositions. You may have used reading plans in the past that were designed to take you through the Bible in a year and so assigned you to read 8 or 10 psalms right in a row each day. When read like this, these psalms probably seemed to say the same thing over and over again, pretty much in the same way. If you really want to appreciate the great breadth and depth of spiritual experience that's expressed in the psalms and the creative variety of the many different forms they take, you can't just plow through the book. This guide will lead you to consider the psalms one at a time, a few in each session, so you can hear the unique and authentic voice of each one. Only in the final session will you then experience the book as a whole.

Lamentations and the Song of Songs are slightly different. While they're also made up of originally independent compositions, these have now been worked together into books that flow smoothly from start to finish. So in sessions 19 and 21 you'll read through these shorter books together in your group and discuss them as a whole.

YOU'LL DECIDE FOR YOURSELVES WHAT TO DISCUSS

In each session of this study guide there are many options for discussion. While a group could complete most sessions in about an hour and a half, any one of the questions could lead to an involved conversation. There's no need to cut the conversation short to try to "get through it all." Group leaders can read through all the questions ahead of time and decide which one(s) to begin with, and what order to take them up in. If you do get into an involved discussion of one question, you can leave out some of the others, or you can extend the study over more than one meeting if you do want to cover all of them.

Note: The first four sessions in this guide are longer because they provide important background material about the three basic types of psalms. Because of their length and significance, you may wish to cover these sessions over the course of more than four meetings.

TOGETHER, YOU'LL RELIVE THE EXPERIENCES OF THE BIBLICAL SONGWRITERS

Each session gives suggestions for how the songs it considers can be read effectively out loud. Many sessions will also invite you to write your own similar compositions, and to sing or listen to songs that are based on the psalms you read, or that have similar messages. In this way you'll be able to relive the experiences the biblical songwriters have expressed in their works. You'll join in the long stream of people, going all the way back to ancient Israel, who've used these timeless songs to express their own spiritual experiences.

EVERYBODY WILL PARTICIPATE

There's plenty of opportunity for everyone to participate, by reading the Scriptures, or by introducing the study or the discussion questions to the group. Leaders can involve quiet people naturally by giving them these opportunities. And everyone will feel they can respond, because the questions aren't looking for "right answers." Instead, they invite people to reflect on deeper issues and pursue an understanding of them together, even if everybody doesn't agree in the end.

YOU'LL ALL SHARE DEEPLY

The discussion questions will invite you to share deeply about your ideas and experiences. The answers to these questions can't be found just by "looking them up." They require reflection on the meaning of each song, in the wider context of the book it belongs to, in light of your personal experience. These aren't the kinds of abstract, academic questions that make the discussion feel like a test. Instead, they'll connect the Bible to your life in practical, personal, relational ways.

To create a climate of trust where this kind of deep sharing is encouraged, here are a couple of ground rules that your group should agree to at its first meeting:

Confidentiality. Group members agree to keep anything that's shared strictly confidential. "What's said in the group stays in the group."

Respect. Group members will treat other members with respect at all times, even when disagreeing over ideas.

HOW TO LEAD GROUP STUDIES USING THIS GUIDE

Each session has three basic parts:

Introduction

Have someone read the introduction to the session out loud for everyone. Then give group members the chance to ask questions about the introduction and to offer their own thoughts and examples. (Occasionally, a discussion question will be suggested just before or after the introduction.)

Reading and Discussion

Most psalms will be introduced with some observations that explain how they're put together and provide some background to the history and culture of the ancient world as it's reflected in them. (When particular terms are introduced that describe the basic types of psalms and the elements commonly found in them, these terms appear in **bold**.) After these observations, there are suggested discussion questions. Many of them have multiple parts that are really just different ways of getting at an issue.

You or a group member can read this background information, and then someone can read the biblical songs for each session out loud. (It's not necessary to read the traditional headings with the psalms.) The study guide will offer suggestions for various ways to do this reading. After each reading, take up whichever discussion questions the group is most interested in.

You don't have to discuss the questions in the order they appear in the study guide. You can choose to spend your time exploring just one or two questions and not do the others. Or you can have shorter discussions of each question so that you do cover them all. As the group leader, before the meeting you should read the questions and the observations that introduce them, and decide which ones you want to emphasize.

As you answer the questions, interact with the observations (you can agree or disagree with them) in light of your reading from the Bible. Use only part of the question to get at the issue from one angle, or use all of the parts, as you choose.

Note: Many of the sessions will suggest songs you can sing or listen to that are based on the psalms. If you want to use these suggestions, look for the songs ahead of time, for example, by finding videos of them on the Internet, getting someone to bring a recorded version of them to your meeting, or having the words and music printed out for people to sing and arranging for someone to play them on a piano or guitar.

For Further Reading and Discussion

At the end of most sessions, other psalms of the type just considered will be listed and described. Your group can discuss some of these if it wants to and has time. Individuals can also read and reflect on them on their own.

TIPS FOR HOME GROUPS, SUNDAY SCHOOL CLASSES, COMMUNITY BIBLE EXPERIENCES, AND INDIVIDUAL USE

If you're using this guide in a *home group*, you may want to begin each meeting (or at least some meetings) by having dinner together. You may also want to have a time of singing and prayer before or after the study. This would be a natural place to use the song suggestions.

If you're using this guide in a *Sunday school class*, you may want to have a time of singing and prayer before or after the study.

This study guide can also be used in connection with a *community Bible experience*. If you're using it in this way:

- Encourage people to read the Scriptures for each session on their own early in the week.
- Do each session together in midweek small groups.
- Invite people to write/create some response to each small-group session that could be shared in worship. In addition to the poems, songs, and illustrations this guide invites people to create, these responses might also include journal or blog entries, dramas, videos, and so on.
- During weekend worship gatherings, give people the opportunity to share their responses, and have preaching on one or more of the Scriptures the community has experienced that week. Speakers can gather up comments they've heard from people and draw on their own reflections as well.
- During the following week the community will then read, discuss, and respond to the Scriptures for the next session, and the worship gathering will once more center around them.
- The experience will culminate with a community reading of the whole book of Psalms, ideally in the context of a one-day retreat. (This is explained in session 24.)

This guide can also be used for *individual study*. You can write out your responses to the questions in a notebook or journal. (However, we really encourage reading and studying the Bible in community!)

Note: Anytime you see *italicized* words in Scripture quotations in this book, the italics have been added for emphasis.

PSALMS ARE THE WORDS TO SONGS

➲ Question for opening discussion: Have you ever liked a song so much that you copied or printed out the words and put them up in your room, posted them on Facebook as a favorite quotation, or did something similar? If so, tell the group what song this was and why you liked it so much.

INTRODUCTION

The psalms are songs that the people of ancient Israel liked so much and sang so often together that their words were written down and collected into a book that became part of the Bible. But we may not realize at first that the psalms are song lyrics, for several reasons.

For one thing, if we've gone to church or read the Bible, we've probably always heard somebody read the psalms out loud, or we've read them silently ourselves. We're not used to singing them or hearing them sung (unless we go to a particular type of church that customarily does this).

For another thing, most of the psalms don't look like the songs we're familiar with today. They don't have the same overall form, and they're written in a different kind of poetry. (But some of the psalms do look pretty much like the songs we know, and we'll be looking at a few of them in this session to show that the psalms really are song lyrics. In the sessions that follow, we'll come to understand and appreciate the many other forms that biblical psalms take.)

Beyond this, many of the psalms have headings that offer a description of when and why they were written. If we read these headings first and try to understand the psalms in light of them, the psalms will seem more like speeches or spoken prayers than songs. For example, the heading to Psalm 52 talks about how King David's enemy Doeg betrayed him, and this psalm sounds like a record of what David said when he publicly confronted Doeg: "Why do you boast of evil, you mighty hero?"

But the headings to the individual psalms actually reflect only a traditional understanding of when they were written. (People who believe that the Bible is the Word of God usually don't consider these headings to be inspired Scripture.) This tradition is accurate in depicting the psalms as coming originally from real-life situations in the lives of people who trusted in God. It's also accurate in suggesting that many of the psalms were written by leading figures in the community of Israel. The psalm headings do tell us reliably how these songs were used in worship (what their tunes were, for example). But we can't be confident that in every case they tell us accurately who wrote a psalm, and when, and why. And so we shouldn't let them lead us to treat the psalms as historical documents that reveal what a given person was saying and thinking at a particular point in their life. Instead, we should appreciate the psalms based on what we can say confidently about them: that they were used in the worship of ancient Israel to help individuals and the community express the thoughts, feelings, questions, and beliefs that arose in the highs and lows of their ongoing relationships with God.

Suppose we didn't know that the song "Take My Hand, Precious Lord" was written by Thomas A. Dorsey in 1932 as a prayer for strength and endurance after his wife and their baby died in childbirth. Suppose we had only an uncertain tradition about who wrote this song and why. But suppose we did still know that Martin Luther King Jr. often had it sung at rallies, to inspire himself and the rest of the civil rights movement. In that case, we would recognize "Take My Hand, Precious Lord" as a song that was the creative, impassioned outpouring of deep faith in some individual's life, which then became part of the spiritual heritage of a community of struggling and triumphant believers. This illustration shows how we can best understand and appreciate the psalms in the Bible.

➲ If you wish, listen to a recording or watch a video of the gospel singer and civil rights leader Mahalia Jackson singing "Take My Hand, Precious Lord," or sing the song together as a group.

READING AND DISCUSSION

Note: The psalm numbers are traditional and are used for convenience in this study guide. The customary order of the psalms is not important for the way they will be approached here. None of the psalmists wrote their compositions with the expectation that they would have a particular location within an eventual collection. The order of the psalms and their division into five books is explained in session 24.

1 Psalm 46 has two 3-line stanzas, a 1-line chorus, another 3-line stanza, a bridge (in which God himself speaks), and a final repetition of the 1-line chorus. Lines of Hebrew poetry usually have two parts and sometimes they have three parts, so these individual poetic lines (such as those below) may look like two or three lines in English translations:

> God is our refuge and strength,
> an ever-present help in trouble.
>
> He says, "Be still, and know that I am God;
> I will be exalted among the nations,
> I will be exalted in the earth."

In most Bibles, the parts of this psalm (stanzas, chorus, bridge) will be set off from one another by some white space. Have someone read Psalm 46 out loud for the rest of the group. (The book of Psalms can be found near the middle of most Bibles.) The reader should pause briefly between each part to emphasize the form of this song.

There are many ways for us to recognize that Psalm 46 is a song. Its heading includes a brief series of instructions for the "director of music." These instructions tell what tune it should be sung to, *Alamoth*. They also tell what kind of composition it is: a *shir* ("song"), as opposed to a *maskil*, a *miktam*, or a *mizmor*, as other psalms are described in their headings. (We don't know exactly what these ancient styles were.) Also, in the original Hebrew, the musical term *selah* appears after the first stanza and after each chorus. This probably indicates that an instrumental interlude was to be played at these points. (Some modern Bibles print the word *selah* where it appears in the psalms, although the NIV does not.)

But the most obvious way to recognize Psalm 46 as a song is from its form. The pattern of stanza, stanza, chorus, stanza, bridge, chorus is familiar to us from songs we know today. This enables us to recognize that this is a musical composition, just as we can recognize a letter by its form or a set of directions by its form. The biblical psalms don't rhyme the way songs today often do, and this might make them seem a little less familiar, but they do have a feature that's very similar to rhyming, and once we learn to recognize it, this will make them feel even more like songs.

Rhyming is based on the repetition of *sound*. Think back to the song "Take My Hand, Precious Lord," if you sang or listened to it a few minutes ago, and recognize the places where one line ends with the same sound as the line before it. (For example, "hand" and "stand.") Hebrew poetry is based instead on the repetition of *meaning*. The second part of a line will re-state what the first part says, draw a contrast to it, or extend it in some way:

He breaks the bow and shatters the spear;
he burns the shields with fire.
(The second part of this line restates the idea in the first part of God destroying weapons of war)

There is a river whose streams make glad the city of God,
the holy place where the Most High dwells.
(The second part expands on the meaning of the "city of God" mentioned in the first part)

As you read and discuss the psalms in the sessions ahead, if you look for this kind of repetition of meaning and think of it as something like rhyming, this will help you engage the psalms as the songs they truly are. (The traditional verse divisions in the Bible don't always correspond with actual lines of Hebrew poetry, so you should use this pattern of repeated meaning to identify poetic lines and not rely on verse numbers.)

➲ What examples can you give of contemporary songs that have verses, a chorus, and a bridge? (*How Great Is Our God* by Chris Tomlin is one example. What others can you think of, whether they're worship songs, popular love songs you might hear on the radio, or some other kind of song?)

➲ We don't know who wrote Psalm 46, or why, but we do know that when they wrote it, they felt as if their world was falling apart. The psalm uses the images of an earthquake, a great storm at sea, and a war to describe the writer's situation. As a group, name some of the things that can happen in a person's life to make them feel this way. When have you felt as if your world was falling apart?

➲ Despite what was happening, the songwriter was very aware of God's presence and wasn't afraid. The writer heard God's voice saying, "Be still." The psalm expresses a confidence that God will bring about a peaceful resolution and make his power and glory known. How can a person listen for and hear God's voice of peace and reassurance in difficult situations? If you've experienced this yourself, share with the group. If you need peace and reassurance in your own life right now, reread Psalm 46 several times in the week ahead and ask God to speak to you through it.

2 Psalms 42 and 43 are actually a single psalm that was later divided into two parts. In *The Books of the Bible* these parts are put back together. (If you're using another edition, it may have a note explaining that they were originally one psalm.) This psalm has three stanzas, and the same chorus appears after each one: "Why, my soul, are you downcast? . . ."

Have someone read Psalms 42 and 43 together out loud. The reader should pause briefly after each stanza and each repetition of the chorus to emphasize the form of this psalm.

⮡ If you've read Psalms 42 and 43 before, tell the group what difference it makes to hear the original whole psalm read aloud with an emphasis on its song form.

⮡ Like the author of Psalm 46, this songwriter is in a very difficult situation. The psalm describes this situation as like being tossed around in huge rapids. If you've ever gone white-water rafting and things nearly got out of control, or if you've been tumbled by a big wave in the ocean, tell the group what this was like. How else does the psalm describe the writer's situation?

⮡ The psalmist asks God, "Why have you forgotten me? Why have you rejected me?" Do you think it's all right with God if we "vent" our feelings to him this way?

⮡ The writer repeatedly tells his soul, which is "downcast" and "disturbed," to have hope and confidence in God. Have you ever been able to find renewed faith in troubling circumstances through this kind of self-talk? If you're facing a difficult situation right now, speak to your own soul in the days ahead, telling it why it should hope in God.

FOR FURTHER READING AND DISCUSSION

• Read Psalm 80 and notice how its form is stanza, chorus, stanza, chorus, stanza, bridge, chorus. What slight change is made in the chorus the second and third time it's repeated? What effect does this change have? This psalm was written after the people of Israel were conquered and carried off into exile. It's a prayer for their restoration. What extended image does the psalm use to describe the nation and its misfortunes? Use this image or a similar one to pray for the spiritual restoration of a nation that's important to you.

- Read Psalm 57 and notice its form: stanza, chorus, stanza, chorus. What difficulty is the songwriter facing? What images does the psalm use to describe this difficulty? How is the emphasis of the second stanza different from the emphasis of the first? How do you think the psalmist was able to experience this change in perspective?

- One clear indication we have that people in ancient Israel used earlier compositions to express their current spiritual experiences is the way Psalm 108 has been put together from the last third of Psalm 57 and the last two-thirds of Psalm 60. Look at these three psalms, and see how this is done. What current compositions do you know that incorporate parts of older songs? (For example, "Grace Like Rain" by Todd Agnew, which includes verses from John Newton's hymn "Amazing Grace.")

PSALMS OF SUPPLICATION: THE BASIC FORM

INTRODUCTION

To illustrate that the psalms were originally songs, in the previous session we considered some psalms that have stanzas and choruses like the songs we know today. But most psalms don't follow this same pattern. Instead, they use some other basic forms that were common in ancient Hebrew songwriting. These forms allow the biblical songwriters to structure a creative expression of the powerful emotions and intense spiritual sensations that arise from their deep experiences with God.

Without some kind of structure to channel all of this energy, these writers would produce something more like an explosion than a coherent expression of their experiences. It would be hard for us today to share meaningfully in a primal scream that was echoing down through the centuries. So it's valuable for the psalmists to have these forms available, and it's valuable for us to understand them.

In other words, learning to recognize and appreciate these forms is important because this helps us understand the purpose of each psalm and appreciate the way it captures the writer's spiritual experiences. This study guide will explain these forms and help you explore the variety of situations they speak to.

The most common type of psalm is a cry for God's help in a time of trouble. About one third of the psalms fit this type. These are often called

psalms of supplication. (The fact that there are so many of these in the Bible suggests that God really does want us to ask for help and doesn't mind when we do.)

But a psalm of supplication isn't essentially about the troubles the writer is experiencing. It's not primarily a prayer for help. Rather, it's a way for the writer to work through a crisis of faith that these troubles have created. The troubles have called God's goodness and power into question. The psalmist wonders, "Does God really care about me? Is God fair? Is God able to help me?" The goal of a psalm of supplication is for the writer to be able to tell God, "I still trust you," despite all the questions the troubles have raised. The psalms in the Bible show people at various stages along the journey towards this goal.

Psalms of supplication are built out of a series of common elements. Not every psalm has all the elements, and the ones that are used can be presented in a variety of orders, but a basic pattern can be recognized. Psalm 54 illustrates this pattern briefly and well:

Cry for Help	Save me, O God, by your name; vindicate me by your might. Hear my prayer, O God; listen to the words of my mouth.
Complaint	Arrogant foes are attacking me; ruthless people are trying to kill me— people without regard for God.
Statement of Trust	Surely God is my help; the Lord is the one who sustains me.
Petition	Let evil recoil on those who slander me; in your faithfulness destroy them.
Vow of Praise	I will sacrifice a freewill offering to you; I will praise your name, LORD, for it is good. You have delivered me from all my troubles, and my eyes have looked in triumph on my foes.

Psalm 54 shows that psalms of supplication typically begin with a **cry for help**. The psalmist calls out to God, begging for rescue in urgent and emotional tones.

A **complaint**, a description of the troubles the writer is facing, usually follows. (This may be combined with the cry for help. A complaint is also known as a lament; some interpreters use the term "lament" to describe this type of psalm as a whole, not just the complaint part.) In Psalm 54, the complaint is about how others are causing trouble. But a complaint may also describe what the writer is experiencing personally or what the community is going through, and so it will say "I" or "we" instead of "they." It may even talk directly to God, saying "you," and complain that God isn't coming to the rescue or that he caused the trouble in the first place. A "you" complaint is known as an **accusation**.

The breakthrough point comes when the psalmist is able to make a **statement of trust** and express confidence in God's goodness and power despite the difficulties.

The psalm will then **petition** or request God to act on the writer's behalf. Within petitions, writers may give reasons why God should rescue them. For example, they're innocent, so they don't deserve to suffer; or they've sinned, but they recognize their fault and are asking for forgiveness. A writer may recall times when God has helped in the past and argue that God should do so again in the present. (This is a **recollection** of God's past mercies to an individual or to the community.) The psalmist may suggest that God's reputation as a righteous judge and dependable deliverer is at stake, and even ask God to destroy the wicked to uphold this reputation.

Psalms of supplication typically end with a **vow of praise**, a promise that the writer will go to the temple and offer a sacrifice to acknowledge God's deliverance. The sacrificed animal will be served to family and friends at a celebration meal where the writer will recount publicly how God came to the rescue. (When giving reasons why God should help them, psalmists may even point out that if they perish, they won't be able to offer this public acknowledgment.) In certain psalms the writer offers some praise in advance.

READING AND DISCUSSION

1 The strong emotions that arise from the psalmists' spiritual experiences have to be given some kind of structure in order to be expressed effectively and meaningfully. By working to understand this structure, we become better able to appreciate and share the experiences that the psalmists are expressing through it. Looking at a number of short psalms of supplication can illustrate their basic pattern and also show how it varies—how these psalms often include some elements but not others and how the elements can be presented in different orders. But our ultimate goal must not be to "analyze" the psalms. (As Robert Frost once noted, poetry can be lost not just in translation but also in interpretation!) Rather, we should seek to experience them as literary creations that express spiritual experiences and that are both songs and prayers.

⮥ Divide your group into teams and have each team look at one or more of the following psalms of supplication. Identify where the elements listed occur within psalm. Then have each team read its psalm(s) aloud to the group, pointing out these elements. If a petition gives reasons why God should help, describe what they are. If there's a complaint, say whether it's an "I/we," "they," or "you" complaint, or some combination of these. Team members should also share their personal responses to the psalms they consider. (As you look at these and other psalms, continue to recognize how Hebrew poetry is based on the repetition of meaning—how the second part of a line restates, contrasts with, or extends what the first part says.)

- Psalm 13: cry for help and complaint; petition; statement of trust; vow of praise
- Psalm 61: cry for help; statement of trust; petition; vow of praise
- Psalm 70: cry for help; petition; cry for help
- Psalm 142: cry for help; statement of trust; complaint; cry for help with statement of trust; petition; vow of praise

➲ Does appreciating the structure of a psalm help you understand it better? If so, explain how.

➲ What contemporary songs or traditional hymns do you know that are like psalms of supplication? (For example, "Lord, Help Me" by Tolu Okeowo.)

➲ Many contemporary worship songs speak of working through troubles to a place where the writer is able to say, "Lord, I know you still *love* me," rather than, "I still know you are a good and powerful God." These songs often express *love for* God, not specifically *trust in* God. How are these songs similar to, and different from, the biblical psalms of supplication?

2 Have someone read Psalm 56 out loud for the group. Then work together to identify these elements in this psalm: cry for help and complaint; statement of trust; complaint; petition; statement of trust; vow of praise.

➲ The psalmist says, "my adversaries . . . twist my words," "they watch my steps" (literally "watch my heels," that is, "look for a way to trip me up"). Have you ever been in a situation where people were twisting your words and trying to trip you up? What kind of fear does a situation like this create?

➲ The psalmist asks God to "list my tears on your scroll" or, in another likely translation, to "put my tears in your wineskin." The image is of God keeping a record of these tears, or even an actual collection of them, to remind him of the psalmist's suffering and need for deliverance. What's it like to think of God as someone who is keenly aware of your tears, even to the point of collecting them to remember how much you need his help?

⮂ Essentially the same statement of trust occurs twice within this psalm. It functions as a chorus between stanzas. (In cases like this, ancient Hebrew songwriting forms converge with the ones we use today.) But there are some subtle differences between the two statements. Identify as many as you can. What is the overall effect of these differences? What change in the psalmist's perspective do they reflect? What do you think brings about this change as the writer composes this psalm?

3 You may recognize by now that Psalm 42–43, which you discussed in the previous session, contains many of the characteristic elements of a psalm of supplication. Look again at this psalm and consider these elements:

- The chorus is a repeated statement of trust (as in Psalm 56).
- The first stanza begins with an expression of desire for God, instead of the usual cry for help. It then includes a complaint and a recollection.
- The second stanza is a further recollection that includes an accusation and a complaint.
- The third stanza is a petition that also includes an accusation but then ends with a vow of praise.

The subtle and masterful blending of these elements gives this psalm its great beauty and power.

⮂ Drawing on what you've learned about psalms of supplication in this session, explain how Psalm 42–43 shows the writer working through a crisis of faith that difficulties have created and reaching a place of renewed trust in God.

⮂ Give people some time to write their own personal psalms of supplication and share them with the group if they're comfortable. Or let them work on this at home and bring them to your next meeting to share. People can use the five common elements illustrated in Psalm 54 as a model and write a psalm that includes each element in the basic order. Or they can choose certain elements and put them in any order they want. The most important thing is to write a psalm that authentically expresses where you are with God in whatever troubles you're currently facing. If you haven't yet worked through to a place of trust, you can leave out the statement of trust, as some psalms do. (Recognize that simply complaining to God expresses some belief that God is willing to listen and may be prepared to act on your behalf.) Those who want to try their hand at Hebrew-style poetry can write two-part lines whose second part repeats, contrasts with, or expands on the first. But it's also fine to write in rhyme or free verse. Songwriters can set their psalms to music.

FOR FURTHER READING AND DISCUSSION

- Read Psalms 3, 4, 5, 27, 28, 64, 74, and 86. Which common elements of psalms of supplication do they use? In what order? What kinds of troubles are the writers facing? How far do they get towards reaffirming their trust in God despite their circumstances?

- Read Psalms 44 and 77 and observe how they include a recollection of God's past mercies to the community and how they appeal to this as grounds to hope that God will help the psalmist in a present difficulty. (The end of Psalm 77 is a symbolic depiction of God parting the Red Sea.) Which of God's past mercies to you, your family, and your community can give you hope and encouragement in your current situation?

PSALMS OF THANKSGIVING: THE BASIC FORM

INTRODUCTION

In the last session we looked at psalms of supplication and saw that they often include a promise to offer a public sacrifice in acknowledgment of God's deliverance. When ancient Israelites went to the temple to offer these sacrifices, they typically sang another kind of psalm at their celebration meal, a **psalm of thanksgiving**. Often they put their personal experiences into words by using timeless songs that others had written. Through continual use, these became part of the community's lasting heritage of worship songs, and they were ultimately gathered into the book of Psalms as we know it today.

But a psalm of thanksgiving isn't primarily a way to say thank you, just as a psalm of supplication isn't primarily a way to ask for help. Instead, a psalm of thanksgiving addresses the same crisis of faith that a psalm of supplication does. The troubles that people experience raise questions about God's goodness and power. And it's not only the person who's in trouble who has these questions. Those around them, looking on, also wonder how God could let this happen. So when a person experiences God's love within a difficult situation and ultimately God's deliverance from that situation, it is their duty and privilege to restore God's reputation in the eyes of those around them.

Psalms of thanksgiving are essentially intended as a public vindication of God's goodness and power.

Like psalms of supplication, psalms of thanksgiving are built out of a number of common elements. They have a basic pattern that is creatively adapted to address various situations. This pattern is illustrated well by Psalm 30.

<table>
<tr><td>Summary Statement</td><td>I will exalt you, LORD,
for you lifted me out of the depths
and did not let my enemies gloat over me.
LORD my God, I called to you for help,
and you healed me.
You, LORD, brought me up from the realm
of the dead;
you spared me from going down to the pit.</td></tr>
<tr><td>Call to Worship</td><td>Sing the praises of the LORD, you his
faithful people;
praise his holy name.
For his anger lasts only a moment,
but his favor lasts a lifetime;
weeping may stay for the night,
but rejoicing comes in the morning.</td></tr>
<tr><td>Description of Troubles</td><td>When I felt secure, I said,
"I will never be shaken."
LORD, when you favored me,
you made my royal mountain stand firm;
but when you hid your face,
I was dismayed.</td></tr>
<tr><td>(includes recollection of
cry for help)</td><td>To you, LORD, I called;
to the Lord I cried for mercy:
"What is gained if I am silenced,
if I go down to the pit?
Will the dust praise you?</td></tr>
</table>

<table>
<tr><td>Song of Victory</td><td>You turned my wailing into dancing;
you removed my sackcloth and clothed me
with joy,
that my heart may sing your praises and not
be silent.</td></tr>
<tr><td>Praise and Thanks</td><td>LORD my God, I will praise you forever.</td></tr>
</table>

As Psalm 30 shows, psalms of thanksgiving often begin with a **summary statement** of how the writer called to God for help and was delivered from trouble. This may be spoken to the people who've gathered around, or it may be addressed directly to God.

These psalms then present a **call to worship** that encourages the family and friends who've gathered for the celebration meal, along with priests from the temple, to join the psalmist in praising God for his deliverance. (The call to worship may also come first, before the summary statement.)

A longer **description of troubles** often follows, explaining in more detail what difficulties the writer faced. This is much like the complaint in a psalm of supplication, except that it's related in the past tense—these troubles are now over. This description typically specifies that in these troubles, the writer called out to God for help.

Then there may be a **song of victory**, describing how God came to the rescue. Sometimes this includes a **theophany**, a vivid depiction of God coming out of heaven to do cosmic battle with his opponents. (There's an extended theophany in Psalm 18, for example.) A primary theme of these theophanies is the recollection of how God parted the waters of the Red Sea to allow the Israelites to escape from slavery in Egypt.

Psalms of thanksgiving typically conclude with expressions of **praise and thanks** to God. A description of the sacrifice and the reason why it's being offered may be included, as in Psalm 66: "I will come to your temple with burnt offerings and fulfill my vows to you—vows my lips promised and my mouth spoke when I was in trouble." Psalm 30 creatively combines the description of

God's deliverance with its expression of praise: it says that God's deliverance *was* to bring the psalmist from a place of despair into a place of worship.

➲ What contemporary songs or traditional hymns do you know that are like psalms of thanksgiving, as they're described here? (For example, the gospel song "Love Lifted Me.")

➲ As we saw in session 2, when psalmists give reasons why God should help them, they often say that if they perish, they won't be able to offer God public praise and vindication. Here in Psalm 30 the writer recalls making this same argument: "What is gained if I am silenced, if I go down to the pit? Will the dust praise you? Will it proclaim your faithfulness?" Do you think God would find this argument convincing? (Followers of Jesus who die go to be in God's presence, and they're able to praise him forever there, so why is it so important for God to be praised and acknowledged here on earth?)

➲ If learning about psalms of thanksgiving has made you realize that God has done something important for you that you've never publicly given him credit for, ask the leaders of your group or church if you can give a public testimony of what God did for you. You may want to do this by writing your own psalm of thanksgiving, using or adapting the basic pattern outlined in this session and reading or singing your psalm for your group or church.

READING AND DISCUSSION

1 Have someone read Psalm 118. It's most likely a thanksgiving for victory over enemies in battle. As a group, notice its elements. It begins with a call to worship and a summary statement, then offers a song of victory. Then there's a description of going through the "gates of the righteous" into the temple to give thanks. After a further depiction of God's deliverance and a call for his continued help, the people who are invited to the meal apparently welcome and bless the psalmist ("Blessed is he who comes in the name of the Lord.") and call for the celebration to begin, saying, "Bind the festal sacrifice with ropes and take it to the horns of the altar." (See the NIV alternative translation. In *The Books of the Bible*, the translators' notes are at the end of the book of Psalms.) This is where the animal will be slain and prepared for the meal. The psalm concludes with praise and another call for thanksgiving.

⮑ What are some good ways for family and friends to encourage people who've experienced God's mercies to share this publicly with others? What kinds of celebrations and ceremonies can they arrange? What role can the listeners play at these events?

2 Have someone read Psalm 116 for the group. Notice how it, too, incorporates the basic elements of a psalm of thanksgiving, but in a slightly different order. It begins with a summary statement and then immediately gives a more detailed description of how the psalmist experienced troubles (apparently a deadly illness) and called on the Lord for help. A song of victory follows, describing how God "delivered . . . from death." The last third of the psalm is an extended depiction of the celebration meal in the temple. The final line is the call to worship. "Praise the Lord" (Hebrew *Hallelu Yah*) is a plural imperative, meaning "*All of you*, praise the Lord (with me)!"

The Lord's Supper, which followers of Jesus observe today, is based on the celebration meals where psalms of thanksgiving were sung (particularly the Passover meal, a special celebration in homes where the Israelites commemorated how God rescued them from slavery in Egypt). Another name for the Lord's Supper, the Eucharist, literally means "thanksgiving." Psalm 116 shows us that like the Lord's Supper, these ancient meals centered around a ceremonial drink, the "cup of salvation" (or "deliverance," that is, the cup in honor of deliverance) and a ceremonial food, the "thank offering," the meat from the sacrificed animal.

⮑ If you're a follower of Jesus and have observed the Lord's Supper regularly, share with the group what it's like to think of it as an occasion to thank God for deliverance from deadly danger and to vindicate God's reputation for power and goodness.

FOR FURTHER READING AND DISCUSSION

- Read Psalms 18, 66, and 138, and identify which common elements of psalms of thanksgiving they use and in what order.
- Psalms 18 and 144 include theophanies (descriptions of God coming in power to the rescue). The one in Psalm 18 is particularly extended. If you're an artist, create an illustration of this theophany and share it with your group. If you don't draw or paint, look online for a photograph or illustration, or choose a photo you've taken yourself that you think is a good depiction of a theophany.

PSALMS OF PRAISE: THE BASIC FORM

INTRODUCTION

The third common type of psalm is the **psalm of praise**. It is built out of two basic elements, a **call to worship** and a **reason to worship**. The reason to worship may be introduced by the words "for" or "because," or with phrases such as "I know" or "know that." A single psalm may present two or more calls to worship, each with its accompanying reasons, and many psalms of praise end with a final call to worship. The basic pattern is illustrated briefly and well by Psalm 117:

Call to Worship	Praise the Lord, all you nations; extol him, all you peoples.
Reason to Worship	*For* great is his love toward us, and the faithfulness of the Lord endures forever.
Call to Worship	Praise the Lord. (*Hallelu Yah*)

Psalms of thanksgiving can also include these two elements. For example, the call to worship in Psalm 30 includes a reason to worship:

Call to Worship	Sing the praises of the Lord, you his faithful people; praise his holy name.

Reason to Worship   *For* his anger lasts only a moment,
but his favor lasts a lifetime;
weeping may stay for the night,
but rejoicing comes in the morning.

But there's an important difference between the two types. Psalms of thanksgiving express the resolution of a crisis of faith, when God's power and goodness have been called into question by troubles, but God has then been vindicated. Psalms of praise represent instead the ideal default state of the faithful believer. They declare a settled confidence that God is on the throne of heaven and all's right with the world, or at least that all will be made right as God's reign is extended farther and farther.

Psalms of praise take up as their themes the very things that troubles can call into question: God's power and goodness. In them, God is praised for his greatness as the Creator of the world and as the ruler of the nations and the leader of the people of Israel, and for his mercy and compassion in delivering, providing for, and preserving those who trust in him.

⮐ What contemporary songs or traditional hymns do you know that are like psalms of praise?

⮐ Have you ever had an experience when you had no really pressing troubles and your spirit naturally turned to worship God? If so, share it with the group.

READING AND DISCUSSION

1 Have someone read Psalm 100 out loud for the group. As you listen, notice that the characteristic pattern of a psalm of praise is repeated twice: there's a call to worship, followed by a reason to worship introduced by "know that," then another call to worship, followed by a reason to worship introduced by "for."

⊃ What different reasons does Psalm 100 give to worship the
Lord? Which ones have to do with God's power, and which ones
have to do with God's goodness?

⊃ Following the basic pattern described in this session, write your
own psalm of praise and set it to music if you're a songwriter.
Share it with your group or in a worship gathering of your church if
you're comfortable doing so.

2 Have someone read Psalm 147 out loud.

⊃ As a group, identify where the three calls to worship and the
three reasons to worship occur in this psalm. (In this case, the
reason sections aren't introduced by words like "for" or "know
that.") Then list all of the individual reasons to worship that are
woven together in each section. Which ones describe God's
greatness as Creator? Which describe God's compassionate care
for the creation? Which speak of God as the ruler of the nations
or as the leader of Israel?

⊃ This psalm concludes by praising God for giving his "laws and
decrees" to the people of Israel. We'll see the theme of God's laws
and teachings taken up in many other psalms. Think about what
the world would be like today if God had never given his laws
to ancient Israel and if their moral imperatives had never been
shared with other nations. Pray together as a group and praise
God for the difference this has made in the world.

3 Have someone read Psalm 103. As you listen, notice how it follows
a simple pattern for a psalm of praise: a call to worship, an extended
reason to worship, then another call to worship. The writer's own person
("soul") is addressed in the opening call, and the whole creation is addressed
in the concluding call.

The general description in the center of this psalm of God's mercy and compassionate care is bracketed by two brief declarations of God's rule: "The Lord works righteousness and justice for all the oppressed"; "The Lord has established his throne in heaven, and his kingdom rules over all." God's enthronement and righteous rule is a dominant theme of praise psalms, as we'll see in later sessions. These two declarations give this psalm another kind of overall shape:

> Call to worship (with description of individual mercies)
>> Declaration of God's reign
>>> Description of God's general mercies
>> Declaration of God's reign
> Call to worship

Compositions built out of paired sections like this are known as *chiasms*. This shape was considered particularly elegant and refined in Hebrew literature.

⮑ The occasion of this psalm is probably the writer's recent recovery from a life-threatening illness. See how this is suggested in the opening call to worship. (There's often a fine line between a psalm of praise and a psalm of thanksgiving, but a given psalm's specific form can help us recognize which kind it is.) This recovery leads the psalmist into a general reflection on the way God "does not treat us as our sins deserve." What character qualities does God have that lead him to act this way, according to this psalm? List as many as you can.

⮑ What statements in Psalm 103 do you find most encouraging personally? Why? How do they speak to your present situation in life or to significant experiences you've had in the past?

FOR FURTHER READING AND DISCUSSION

• Read Psalms 95, 98, 135, and 149 and identify the call to worship and reason to worship sections in each psalm. Which reasons are introduced by words or phrases such as "for" or "know that," and which aren't? Which describe God's power as Creator of the world, ruler of the nations, or leader of Israel? Which describe God's goodness in caring for the creation or in protecting, preserving, and providing for those who trust in him? (Remember that the goal of trying to recognize the forms of the different types of psalms is to become better able to appreciate and share the experiences that the psalmists are expressing through them.)

PSALMS THAT COMBINE THE BASIC FORMS

INTRODUCTION

As we've noted, the three forms that psalms typically take (supplication, thanksgiving, praise) provide the biblical songwriters with a basic structure for the creative expression of the powerful emotions and intense spiritual sensations that arise from their deep experiences with God. But the psalmist's responses to their experiences are often so creative that they actually transform the very literary forms that are supposed to structure them. Psalmists can adapt or combine different forms into something new that doesn't quite fit any of the categories we've described in the previous sessions. This should not surprise us. Creative expression can't be restricted to tightly defined forms. The last thing we want to do is "classify" the psalms, rather than understand, appreciate, enjoy, and be moved by them.

In this session we'll look at some of the psalms that adapt or combine the forms we've learned about, in order to appreciate the creativity and vitality behind all of these musical expressions of spiritual experience in the Bible.

READING AND DISCUSSION

1 Have someone read Psalm 33 out loud for the group.

This psalm begins and develops like a psalm of praise. There's a call to worship, followed by a reason to worship introduced by "for." The reason to worship describes the Lord as the righteous ruler of the world, as the powerful Creator, as the commander of the destinies of the nations, and as the leader of Israel. We would expect a psalm of praise like this to culminate in a final call to worship. But instead, Psalm 33 then talks about how only God can truly deliver, and it concludes with a statement of trust and a petition. While it begins as a psalm of praise, it ends as a psalm of supplication.

We can infer from what the psalmist says that the country is at war, likely trying to repel a foreign invasion, since the people are threatened by "famine" and "death." But this does not provoke a crisis of faith for the psalmist. Rather than asking how God can allow this or accusing God of abandoning his people, the writer's faith remains firm and settled, so that the psalm asserts God's authoritative rule, and it petitions for deliverance from a stance of trust and confidence. The occasion calls for a psalm of supplication, but the writer's response to it is best expressed in a psalm of praise, so the two forms are creatively combined.

⇒ Have you ever had an experience when a difficult or dangerous trial didn't raise questions for you about God's goodness or power, and you were able to face it with confident faith and "wait in hope for the Lord"? If so, tell the group about this experience.

2 Take turns reading Psalm 107 out loud. One person can start, and then a new reader should begin each time the psalm starts to describe the experiences of a different group. (These descriptions begin with "Some wandered," "Some sat in darkness," etc. The last one begins, "He turned rivers into a desert." The person who takes this part should read all the way to the end of the psalm.)

Psalm 107 is essentially a psalm of thanksgiving. It's written to celebrate the return of the Israelites from exile, as its opening states. Like a typical thanksgiving psalm, it recounts a deliverance from troubles that are now in the past, and it describes a public acknowledgment of God through the "sacrifice" of "thank offerings" in the "assembly of the people."

But Psalm 107 is also unlike typical thanksgiving psalms in many ways. It doesn't ask others to join in celebrating a deliverance that the writer has experienced personally. Instead, it asks them to recognize how they've been delivered themselves and to thank God for that.

In its form, it's more like a psalm of praise. After an opening call to worship, it gives a series of reasons to worship, and each one concludes with another call to worship. These are all worded very similarly and function as a repeated chorus after each stanza of this song. But the psalm is actually presenting calls and reasons to "give thanks," rather than to "praise the Lord." And the reasons for thanks are specific deliverances that various groups of people have experienced, rather than aspects of God's objective power and goodness. So this is a true blending of the thanksgiving and praise forms.

In effect, the return from exile inspires this writer to think of many different groups of people whom God faithfully rescues in the course of life, and to issue a call for all of them to join in giving "thanks to the Lord for his unfailing love and his wonderful deeds for mankind." Only a combination of two forms can effectively express what's in this writer's heart.

⮌ Which of the following groups that are named in Psalm 107 do you identify with? What experiences have you had that are like theirs, and how have you seen God work in these experiences?

- People who are "lost" and can't find their way "home." The specific reference in this psalm is probably to caravans crossing the desert, but this category also includes anyone who's "lost" in life.
- "Prisoners" in "darkness." This could include actual prison inmates, as well as anyone who's held prisoner by things like depression, addiction, etc.
- People who are gravely ill.
- Fishers and sailors at risk on the ocean, and more broadly anyone who feels as if they're tossed by violent storms in life and at risk of "drowning."
- Farmers depending on a good harvest, and anyone who has to cultivate a project over the long term.

Once everyone has shared, pray together as a group and give thanks to God for his "unfailing love" and the "wonderful deeds" you've seen him do in situations like these.

FOR FURTHER READING AND DISCUSSION

• Read Psalm 40 and observe that it's made up of a fully formed psalm of thanksgiving, followed by a fully formed psalm of supplication. (Identify the elements in each one.) The supplication section has been carefully crafted to fit together with the thanksgiving section, intentionally echoing its language in several places. It appears that a psalmist who came to the temple to celebrate a recent deliverance was also facing a new trouble, and so used the occasion of thanking God to make a renewed petition for help.

⮌ Have you ever emerged from one difficult situation, only to find yourself plunged into another? Were you able to take courage from the thought that the same God who delivered you from the first difficulty was still with you in the second one? (Can this thought encourage you now?)

PSALMS THAT EXPAND ONE ELEMENT WITHIN A FORM

INTRODUCTION

We saw in the previous session that the psalmists sometimes combine the basic forms in order to express their spiritual experiences more effectively. But the primary way in which the psalmists creatively adapt the basic forms is by expanding one particular element within them, so that it determines a psalm's overall shape and meaning. In certain cases it can crowd out all of the other elements and make up the entire psalm.

We've already seen something of this process in earlier sessions. As you looked at a group of short supplication psalms in session 2, you saw how certain elements can be omitted from the basic form and others expanded. In the further reading and discussion section of session 3, you saw a brief theophany in Psalm 144 and an expanded one in Psalm 18 that makes up a significant portion of that psalm. In this session we'll look at this process in more detail. In the following sessions, we'll look at the kinds of psalms that are created when certain elements of the basic forms are greatly expanded to develop specific themes and speak to particular situations in life.

READING AND DISCUSSION

1 We saw in session 2 that psalms of supplication can include a **claim of innocence** among the reasons they give why God should deliver the psalmist. Have someone read Psalm 17 out loud and notice how it includes these basic elements: cry for help, claim of innocence, statement of trust and petition for help, complaint (description of troubles—in this case, enemies), another petition for help, and a final statement of trust and confidence in God. Then have someone read Psalm 26 and notice how this entire psalm is essentially a claim of innocence, with only the whisper of a cry for help at the beginning and of a vow of praise at the end.

Troubling situations in the life of a person of faith call for self-examination. They raise questions such as, "Did I get into this situation because I wasn't walking closely with God and strayed off the right path?" and even "Is God punishing me because I did something wrong?" These questions must be faced honestly and responsibly before a person can credibly ask God for help. In many psalms, such as Psalm 17, we have briefer indications that the psalmist has asked these questions and answered them satisfactorily. But in Psalm 26 we have an enlarged snapshot of the moment when a person emerges from the exercise of self-examination to declare confidently that they haven't brought their troubles on themselves through disobedience or neglect of God's ways, and so they expect God to deliver them.

Psalmists who make claims of innocence like this aren't asserting that they're entirely sinless. Rather, they describe themselves as *tam* (NIV "blameless"), meaning that they aren't consciously doing anything that they know is wrong, and as *tsedeq* (NIV "just"), meaning that they've faithfully fulfilled their responsibilities to God and neighbor. They're saying that they've chosen to follow the general way of life that characterizes the righteous, rather than the way of the wicked. (We'll learn much more about these two "ways" when we consider the wisdom psalms in session 16.)

⟳ Do you think a person today could realistically conclude that they haven't caused their own troubles by straying from the right path and that they can expect God's deliverance because they aren't consciously doing anything they know is wrong?

➲ The author of Psalm 17 tells God, "My steps have held to your paths," literally "to your tracks." The image is of God leading the way and the psalmist stepping right where God put his own feet. Has God been laying out "tracks" for you to follow? How well are you doing at placing your feet in them?

2 Have someone read Psalm 96. Notice how it follows the most basic pattern of a psalm of praise: call to worship, reason to worship introduced by "for," call to worship. But in this case the concluding call to worship, which in other psalms can be as short as a single line (*Hallelu Yah*, "Praise the Lord"), expands to fill the entire second half, so that the reason to worship is only one quarter of the psalm.

Then have someone read Psalm 148. Notice its pattern: call to worship, reason to worship introduced by "for," call to worship, reason to worship introduced by "for" (with *Hallelu Yah* at the beginning and end). The calls to worship once again make up the bulk of this psalm. It explains briefly *why* God should be worshipped—as the Creator and as Israel's deliverer (the image of the "horn" refers to strength and military victory). But its essential focus is on *who* should worship. The first half begins, "Praise the Lord from the heavens" and then calls upon the angels and the sun, moon, stars, and sky to worship God. The second half begins, "Praise the Lord from the earth" and calls upon natural forces, features of the landscape, and plants, animals, and humans to worship God.

Finally, have someone read Psalm 150. See how the call to worship takes over this entire psalm—basically no reason to worship is given. Instead, the psalmist calls on the various instruments in the ancient musician's repertoire, and finally on "everything that has breath," to praise the Lord.

➲ What contemporary songs or traditional hymns do you know that are almost entirely calls to worship?

➲ What do you picture when you think about all of creation praising God together?

➲ If you wish, conclude your time together by singing, listening to, or watching Matt Redman's song "Let Everything That Has Breath," which is inspired by Psalm 150 and develops many of the themes we've seen in praise psalms. ("Praise You in the heavens, joining with the angels . . . Praise You on the earth now, joining with creation.")

FOR FURTHER READING AND DISCUSSION

- Read Psalm 114 and notice that, by contrast, it's a psalm of praise that consists almost entirely of a reason to worship: God's deliverance of Israel from slavery in Egypt. There's only a hint of a call to worship at the end, when the psalm says, "Tremble, earth, at the presence of the Lord." In later sessions you'll consider more praise psalms that basically give reasons to worship, with no calls to worship.

- Read Psalm 52 and notice that it consists almost entirely of the condemnation of a wicked man. Many supplication psalms include a call for the destruction of the wicked to show that the psalmist longs for God's justice. We've already seen some briefer examples of this (for example, in Psalm 28), but in the case of Psalm 52, the condemnation is expanded and takes up almost the entire psalm. In session 10 we'll look at more psalms like this.

PSALMS OF SUPPLICATION WITH AN EXPANDED STATEMENT OF TRUST

Psalms of Trust

INTRODUCTION

When the statement of trust in a supplication psalm expands and displaces most of the other elements, a psalm of trust is created. While troubles may still be perceptible in the background, these psalms are essentially calm, stately affirmations of reliance on God by writers who have worked through whatever crisis of faith their troubles may have generated. Psalm 46 (which we considered in session 1), with its repeated assertion that "the LORD Almighty is with us; the God of Jacob is our fortress," is a good example of a psalm of trust.

READING AND DISCUSSION

1 One of the simplest and most beautiful psalms of trust is Psalm 131. Have someone read it aloud for the group.

⮑ A weaned child is one who is no longer nursing, but who may still rest quietly in its mother's bosom because being in her presence is so peaceful. What is it like to use this image to think about calming and quieting your soul before God?

⮌ Are you concerning yourself with "great matters" that are "too wonderful" for you? Which things in your life right now are your responsibility to address, and which are beyond you and can only be entrusted to God?

2 Have someone read Psalm 139. The author of this psalm is troubled by wicked enemies and so enters a process of soul-searching and self-examination that leads to the realization, "*You* have searched *me*, Lord." While the writer does pray at the end for the destruction of these enemies and asks God for help in self-examination, most of this psalm is an extended, rapturous meditation on how God knows everything we're thinking and doing, and how he watches over us throughout our lives, day and night, wherever we may be.

⮌ Find out who in your group has been the deepest underground, the highest in the air, the longest in the dark, and the farthest away from your current location. Then give thanks together as a group that none of these people was any farther from the presence of God than a person in the most sacred worship space you can imagine.

⮌ What do you believe God was thinking as he watched you take shape in your mother's womb? What great days was God ordaining for you to live out even then?

3 In Psalm 91, the troubles and dangers, and the need to call on God for rescue, are in the foreground, not the background. But the whole psalm is nevertheless a serene and confident affirmation of God's protection and care, with the Lord himself speaking at the end to promise deliverance to all who call on him. Have someone read this psalm aloud for the group.

⮌ Have you ever felt God give you the assurance he'd protect you from danger at a particular time or in a particular place? If so, tell the group about this. Why is it that people sometimes do suffer harm or injury even when they're faithfully following God?

4 The best-known psalm of trust, and indeed the most beloved of all the psalms, is Psalm 23. Read this psalm out loud all together (in unison).

Psalm 23 is traditionally attributed to David. While we can't be entirely confident of the traditions that grew up around all the psalms regarding their authors, in this case the tradition seems to be well-founded. David was a shepherd before he became Israel's king. From his own experience tending sheep, and with his songwriting ability, he would have been able to develop this marvelous extended image of the Lord as his own shepherd—providing for him, guiding him, protecting him, and enjoying his company. Even though it briefly mentions enemies and the danger of death (NIV "darkest valley" is literally the "valley of the shadow of death"), this psalm is primarily an expression of peaceful, confident trust in the divine shepherd's loving, watchful care.

⮑ If you've ever cared for sheep or seen someone care for them, or if you've read a book such as Philip Keller's *A Shepherd Looks at Psalm 23*, explain what a shepherd has to do to provide sheep with clean water, safe pasture, and protection from predators. In a modern, urban, industrial society, what figure corresponds most closely to a shepherd?

⮑ What about the Lord as your shepherd is most meaningful to you right now? Why?

   a. He provides for me.

   b. He guides me.

   c. He protects me.

   d. He enjoys my company.

⮑ Many songs and hymns have been based on Psalm 23 over the years, including "The Lord's My Shepherd, I'll Not Want" in the 1650 *Scottish Psalter* (often sung to the tune "Brother James' Air"), "The King of Love My Shepherd Is" by Henry Baker (1868), "The New 23rd" by Ralph Carmichael (1969), "The Lord is My Shepherd" by Keith Green (1982), and "Psalm 23" by Jason

Upton (2002). Which one is your favorite, and why? Sing a version together in your group, or watch a video of one online.

FOR FURTHER READING AND DISCUSSION

- Read Psalms 16, 62, and 63. These are other examples of psalms of trust. How do they encourage you to "trust in him at all times . . . for God is our refuge"?

PSALMS OF SUPPLICATION FOR HEALING OF SICKNESS

INTRODUCTION

Many of the psalms of supplication ask God to heal the psalmist from a grave illness. In these psalms the complaint may be greatly expanded. The writers describe in evocative imagery what it's like to be severely afflicted in body, to have their friends avoid and desert them, to have their enemies gloat over their condition and look forward to their death, and to feel that God is punishing them through their sickness.

Down through the centuries faithful people suffering from serious illnesses have found great encouragement in these psalms. They show that others who've trusted in God have also gone through the experience of sickness. They model an honest expression to God of the agony and despair that disease can cause. And ultimately they demonstrate that faith and hope can remain strong even when the body is weak.

READING AND DISCUSSION

1 Have someone read Psalm 102, and notice its elements as a psalm of supplication: opening cry for help; complaint; statement of trust; vow of praise; petition. This psalm was composed some time after the Babylonians destroyed Jerusalem. It compares the writer's experience of sickness to the wasted state of the city and prays that God will both "rebuild Zion" and "respond to the prayer of the destitute."

⊃ How do the images in the complaint capture the experience of prolonged illness? Draw on your own times of sickness, or those of people you know, to identify the various aspects of this experience as they're depicted in Psalm 102 (physical pain, loss of appetite, isolation, etc.).

⊃ The psalmist appeals to God, "Do not take me away . . . in the midst of my days." The argument seems to be, "God, your 'years go on through all generations,' but you have to appreciate the brevity of human life; don't 'cut short my days,' since they're already so few." Do you think God would be moved by an appeal like this?

⊃ Psalm 102 expresses the hope that the writer's experience will be an encouragement "for a future generation, that a people not yet created may praise the LORD." The psalmists recognize how the people of their time are using earlier songs to express their spiritual experiences, and they hope that people of later times will be able to use their own compositions in the same way. As you consider several psalms that are prayers for healing in this session, see if they can help you speak to and pray for your own situation and that of your loved ones.

2 Have someone read Psalm 88. Notice that after an opening cry for help, the rest of the psalm consists of an expanded complaint, without a statement of trust or even a petition.

⊃ The author of this psalm has suffered from a lifelong illness ("from my youth") without any relief. Instead of a petition, the psalm describes how the writer's prayers for healing have gone unanswered. The psalmist feels totally abandoned and forgotten.

This is one of the darkest psalms in the Bible. What is the value of giving a voice within the Scriptures to this kind of experience?

➲ Instead of a vow of praise, the psalm argues that the writer, if not healed, won't be able to praise God from the grave, from the "land of oblivion." The perspective is that this earth is a place where God's power and goodness are experienced in a unique way, and so it's vitally important for them to be appreciated and acknowledged here. If we approached life more from this perspective, do you think we would pray more fervently for divine deliverances, rather than taking comfort in the thought that anything we might suffer on earth will be made up to us in the next life?

3 Have someone read Psalm 38 and notice that it, too, consists almost entirely of a complaint, except for a brief statement of trust and a concluding cry for help.

➲ What further aspects of the experience of physical suffering does Psalm 38 depict? How?

➲ In this case the suffering is due to something the psalmist has done wrong. (We're not told specifically what this was.) In addition to physical pain, the psalmist feels crushed by the weight of guilt. Describe some ways in which a person today might experience illness or injury because of their own wrong choices. What hope or encouragement could a person like this find in Psalm 38?

4 Have someone read Psalm 22 for the group. Observe that after an opening cry for help and a statement of trust, there's an expanded complaint, and then, after a brief petition, there's an extended vow of praise.

➲ What aspects of the experience of serious illness does Psalm 22 depict? Particularly note aspects you didn't see depicted in the earlier psalms in this session.

⮑ Psalm 22 makes a more extensive vow of praise than any other psalm. It envisions people all over the earth, rich and poor, present and future, hearing the psalmist's account of God's deliverance and rejoicing together. How do you think this psalmist, who was suffering so severely, was able to envision such a glorious outcome?

NOTE

Many interpreters have noticed a strong similarity between the sufferings described in Psalm 22 and the experience of crucifixion, which was unknown in these times. They've wondered whether the writer was given an advance glimpse of Jesus' sufferings on the cross. What we can say for certain is that Jesus consciously used the words of Psalm 22 to describe his own sufferings. When he cried out, "My God, my God, why have you forsaken me?" he was referring to all of Psalm 22 by quoting its first line. (This was how the Jews of his time identified individual psalms). This shows that Jesus identified deeply with all human suffering, including all the aspects of lingering illness, when he came to earth and gave his life as the Savior and Healer of the world.

Psalms that Jesus and the early community of his followers used to express his experiences on earth and to describe his role as the Messiah, God's supreme deliverer, are known as **Messianic psalms**. Psalm 118, which we considered in session 3, is another good example of this kind of psalm. When Jesus traveled to Jerusalem for the festival of Passover one year, the crowds greeted him in the words of Psalm 118, saying, "Blessed is he who comes in the name of the Lord!" They did this to show that they believed he was not just someone who was celebrating God's past deliverances with them, but someone who was bringing a new kind of deliverance as the Messiah. Shortly afterwards, Jesus himself quoted another part of Psalm 118 to assert that he was the Messiah: "The stone the builders rejected has become the cornerstone; the Lord has done this and it is marvelous in our eyes." Psalm 41, considered just below, is also Messianic. Jesus said its description of betrayal by a friend was fulfilled when Judas betrayed him.

The Messianic psalms are a special case within a general pattern. While the people of Israel looked back to earlier songs to express their spiritual experiences, the psalms themselves also look forward: their authors, as we've just seen, hoped they would be used by later generations. We can and should use them this way today. And we can also see from the Messianic psalms that Jesus fulfilled the vision of those who, like the author of Psalm 102, looked ahead to a day when all "peoples and kingdoms" would "assemble to worship the LORD," drawn together by God's supreme deliverance.

FOR FURTHER READING AND DISCUSSION

- Read Psalms 6, 31, 41, and 71 and recognize how they are psalms of supplication for healing of sickness. Note their elements, particularly how the complaint is expanded. Use them to put into words the experiences and hopes of people you know who are suffering from illness. There are many of these prayers for healing among the psalms—God knows we need them!

PSALMS OF SUPPLICATION FOR DELIVERANCE FROM ENEMIES

INTRODUCTION

Other psalms of supplication ask God to deliver the writer from powerful and malicious enemies. In these psalms the petition or the complaint may be greatly expanded. The psalmists describe both the external dangers that threaten them and their internal feelings of anxiety and fear. These psalms voice the desperate pleas of the hunted for escape from their pursuers and capture the harrowing emotions of people whom others are trying to harm and destroy.

READING AND DISCUSSION

1 Have someone read Psalm 59 out loud. Notice that it's largely a petition for deliverance that includes a complaint, but that it also has a chorus, repeated twice, that culminates each time in a statement of trust. (The chorus begins, "They return at evening, snarling like dogs" and ends, "You are . . . my God on whom I can rely.")

The traditional heading of Psalm 59 says that David wrote it when Saul, his predecessor as king of Israel, was trying to kill him. But if this tradition is accurate, then the psalm was later adapted to be used as a prayer for Israel's deliverance from enemy armies, which it refers to as "the nations." The likely setting for the final form of the psalm is an occasion when a hostile coalition attacked Israel to try to get plunder, even though it hadn't violated any agreements. The king is petitioning God on behalf of all the people.

⮑ The primary image in this psalm is a portrayal of the enemies as a pack of ravenous wild dogs. Have you ever been threatened or attacked by a dog or a pack of dogs? If so, explain why a songwriter would use this image to describe enemies.

⮑ How does the writer work through to a place of trust and confidence by the end of this psalm? Where does the psalmist find assurance that God will help?

⮑ If you've been in a country or region that was being attacked by an army or militia, or if someone you know has been, describe what this was like. Pray together for nations and groups that are being attacked in this way.

2 The specific situation behind Psalm 55 is harder to identify, because this psalm focuses on the writer's inner anguish in the face of an enemy's insults, threats, and attacks. It is clear that a former friend, who claims to be a person of faith, is being deceitful and going back on promises. This is happening against a background of spreading social disintegration in the city, which is perhaps encouraging people like the former friend to believe they can get away with deception and betrayal. Have someone read Psalm 55 for the group and note that it is largely a complaint, primarily a description of the psalmist's internal distress, but that it also offers some strong statements of trust.

⮑ Have you ever been deceived and betrayed by someone you thought you could trust as a friend and fellow believer? Without naming any names, share with the group what this experience was like. Did you find that you could "cast your cares on the LORD" in this situation?

⊃ More generally, have you ever been in a hostile situation that you just wanted to escape from ("flee far away"), but you couldn't? (For example, bullying at school or in the workplace.) If you prayed for help within this situation and you feel that God heard and answered you, tell the group how.

3 The language of Psalm 35 suggests that its author is the object of a lawsuit. (A *rîb* was a formal accusation in ancient Israel that someone hadn't honored the legal and financial obligations of a covenant, a solemn agreement, that they'd made with another person.) The psalm uses legal language in several places, for example, when it asks God to deliver a verdict in the writer's favor ("vindicate me"). The psalmist is being accused by "ruthless witnesses" and faces "false accusations," but is "poor and needy" and so doesn't have the resources to fight back alone. To add insult to injury, the people bringing the lawsuit are apparently well known to the psalmist, who has actually helped them in the past.

Have someone read Psalm 35 out loud for the group. Notice that it consists almost entirely of a petition for deliverance from enemies, with only brief vows of praise in the middle and at the end. A description of the troubles these enemies are causing is worked into the extended petition.

⊃ Have you, or has someone you know, ever been involved in a lawsuit? Was the other party a formerly close friend or relative? What was at risk if the suit was decided in the opponent's favor? What fears and anxieties did this create? How did things turn out in the end? Did you, or the person you know, experience God's presence and assurance during the proceedings? If so, explain in what way. How could Psalm 35, or a petition to God like it, help and encourage a person involved in a court case?

⊃ Even if you haven't been to court, have people ever made "false accusations" against you, insisting, "With our own eyes we have seen it"? How can people who've been falsely accused defend themselves? If God acted to "vindicate" them, what would this look like?

➲ Pray together as a group for justice to be done and the truth to be known in formal accusations and legal proceedings that you're aware of and concerned about.

FOR FURTHER READING AND DISCUSSION

- Psalms 7, 9–10, 12, and 143 are other psalms of supplication for deliverance from enemies. (Like Psalm 42–43, Psalm 9–10 was originally a single psalm that was later separated into two parts.) Read through these psalms, and notice how each one is shaped overall by its petition for deliverance. Use them to help you reach a place of trust in God as you face enemies yourself and as you seek to help others who are being deceived, betrayed, or attacked.

PSALMS OF SUPPLICATION THAT CALL FOR THE DESTRUCTION OF THE WICKED

Imprecatory Psalms

INTRODUCTION

Sometimes psalmists who are troubled by wicked enemies become concerned not only for their own survival but for the LORD's reputation as a God who upholds justice. If treacherous people succeed and prosper, others may question whether God is good and powerful enough to maintain justice—to vindicate the righteous and thwart the wicked. These others may then choose the way of the wicked themselves, and the entire society will become violent and corrupt. So a psalm of supplication for deliverance from enemies may include a call for God to destroy the wicked. This is known as an **imprecation**. The psalmist isn't asking for revenge, but for God to demonstrate his justice. In an **imprecatory psalm**, this call expands and becomes the major element of the composition.

We've already encountered briefer imprecations in a number of other psalms. For example, Psalm 17 tells God, "May what you have stored up for the wicked fill their bellies; may their children gorge themselves on it, and may there be leftovers for their little ones." Psalm 139, a psalm of trust, includes this imprecation: "If only you, God, would slay the wicked! . . . Do I not hate those who hate you, LORD?" As these examples show, the language of an imprecation can be very severe, and raise troubling questions for followers of Jesus today. (Should children be punished for their parents' sins? Didn't Jesus say we shouldn't hate other people, that this was as bad as murder?) As we consider the imprecatory psalms in this session and see extended examples of this kind of language, we'll work to understand what place they have in God's Word.

READING AND DISCUSSION

1 Psalm 58 is a psalm of supplication for deliverance from enemies, unjust rulers who are oppressing the people. It consists almost entirely of a complaint and a petition for deliverance, in the form of an imprecation. The goal of the imprecation is to vindicate God's moral government of the world. The psalmist wants to see these oppressive rulers punished so that people will say, "Surely the righteous still are rewarded; surely there is a God who judges the earth." Have someone read Psalm 58 for the group.

➲ This psalm suggests that these rulers have become intractably evil: they're like a cobra that has "stopped its ears" and "will not heed the tune of the charmer." If you knew that a leader who was brutally oppressing a society or nation was never going to change, would you be comfortable praying that God would remove them from power, even if this meant they would be violently overthrown and killed?

➲ Instead of a vow of praise, Psalm 58 ends by anticipating how the righteous will rejoice "when they are avenged." It depicts the righteous garishly celebrating their own deliverance by "dipping their feet in the blood of the wicked." Do you feel that a celebration like this could honor God's justice in some cases? If so, can you give some examples from history or literature of similar celebrations (that may or may not involve actually bathing in blood) that you feel are appropriate and justified in their circumstances?

2 Psalm 109 includes many of the common elements of a psalm of supplication (cry for help, complaint, petition, vow of praise), but the petition makes up most of the psalm and includes a lengthy imprecation. Have someone read this psalm out loud.

Once again the reason for asking God to destroy the wicked is to vindicate his justice, to demonstrate that he "stands at the right hand of the needy, to save their lives from those who would condemn them." But this psalmist ironically asks God to use *injustice* to destroy his wicked enemy. This includes injustice in the sense of the legal process being subverted ("appoint someone evil to oppose my enemy" in court) and injustice in the sense of not caring for the poor and needy ("may no one . . . take pity on his fatherless children"). But this will actually be an expression of *retributive justice* (that is, payback: "an eye for an eye and a tooth for a tooth"). Because this enemy "hounded to death the poor and the needy and the brokenhearted," and made their survivors destitute, the psalmist asks God to do the same to him.

⮑ Say whether you agree or disagree with the following statement and why: "The world is a tightly-woven web of relationships. Everything that affects one person affects other people as well, particularly those closest to them. So we can't ask God to judge and punish wrongdoers without expecting that this will affect their families too."

⮑ Does retributive justice demonstrate that God is a just God, even though it might seem to be unfair to people who suffer because their wicked family members are punished?

⮑ Do you know any followers of Jesus who are working to help the families of prison inmates, the survivors of criminals or gang members who've met violent deaths, etc.? If so, tell the group what they're doing.

3 Have someone read Psalm 11 for the group. This psalm says that "the Lord examines the righteous, but the wicked, those who love violence, he hates with a passion." (Literally "his soul hates them.") This kind of righteous hatred is a strong negative feeling towards evil that makes someone want to have nothing to do with it. It's not a deep-seated bitterness that makes them committed to doing everything they can to ruin someone else's life. But the imprecatory psalms show that "hatred" as a repulsion from evil can lead someone to ask God to destroy the wicked in order to end their violent oppression of others.

⮑ What do you think of the idea that it's all right for us to feel hatred, as an emotion, for the evil things that people do and for how these things affect others? How can we keep this emotion from becoming bitterness or a desire for revenge rather than justice?

⮑ Have you ever been hurt by someone badly enough that you wanted the other person to pay, and it took a lot of time and prayer for you to get to a place of forgiveness? (Or maybe you haven't been able to forgive yet.) How do you think God wants us to pray when we're that hurt? What place, if any, is there for expressing not-entirely-righteous anger in prayer?

⮑ Would you be comfortable with the idea of God "hating" if this meant not that God detests certain people intrinsically, but rather that God is strongly repulsed by injustice and oppression, and by people when they practice these things?

FOR FURTHER READING AND DISCUSSION

Read and discuss these imprecatory psalms:

- Psalm 140. Identify the elements of this psalm of supplication. Where is the imprecation? Where does the psalmist talk about God's reputation being upheld?
- Psalm 141. The psalmist prays, "Do not let my heart be drawn to what is evil so that I take part in wicked deeds." How does this prayer relate to the purpose of imprecations?

- Psalm 83. This is a prayer for national deliverance from invading enemy armies. The psalmist asks God to defeat them "so that they will seek your name" and know "that you alone are the Most High over all the earth." How might their defeat accomplish this?

- Psalm 69. This psalmist says, "Do not let [my enemies] share in your salvation. May they be blotted out of the book of life." Is there ever a place for us to ask that some people will be excluded from God's presence? Could this vindicate God's justice?

- Psalm 137. This psalm concludes with a horrifying celebration of Babylonian infants being "dashed against the rocks." The Babylonians apparently did this to Israelite infants when they destroyed Jerusalem, so this is probably a cry for retributive justice. But is it going too far?

PSALMS OF SUPPLICATION FOR THE FORGIVENESS OF SIN

Penitential Psalms

INTRODUCTION

Psalms of supplication are a means to ask for help and ultimately to trust God in times of trouble. But sometimes the primary trouble is the psalmist's own sin. The writer is guilty of a serious breach of God's ways that has harmed and defrauded others. While this sin may be considered responsible for further troubles (sickness, triumph of enemies, etc.), these are secondary issues. What the psalmist wants and needs most is deliverance from the weight of guilt and shame and the restoration of God's customary favor and presence. In pursuit of these things, the writer confesses the sin and pleads for forgiveness. These acts can color every element of a psalm of supplication so that it becomes what's known as a **penitential psalm**. (Penitence means sorrowing over sin and taking responsibility for it.) In this case, it's not the expansion of one element, but the way one theme pervades every element, that creates a distinct kind of psalm.

READING AND DISCUSSION

1 Psalm 51 is a fully formed psalm of supplication whose every element is colored by the theme of penitence. Have someone read it for the group, and note its elements:

- The opening cry is for mercy and forgiveness, not for rescue from some other trouble.

- Instead of a claim of innocence as a reason why God should help, there's an extended admission of guilt.

- The petition is directly for forgiveness.

- The vow of praise includes a promise to proclaim how God has forgiven and to encourage others to confess their own sins. It also makes clear that the writer isn't counting on an animal sacrifice itself to win renewed acceptance, but rather on a "broken spirit" and a "contrite heart" as the sacrifices that are truly acceptable to God.

⮑ Penitential psalms like this one describe the physical, emotional, and spiritual symptoms of guilt, including sorrow, depression, fatigue, physical aches, sleeplessness, and a sense of distance from God. At times when you've needed to make something right with God or other people, have you experienced symptoms like these? Without revealing the specifics of your situation, describe how you felt until you were able to make things right.

2 Psalm 32 shows that the themes of confession and forgiveness can also pervade every element of a psalm of thanksgiving and transform it into a penitential psalm. Have someone read this psalm for the group, and once again note its elements:

- The opening is a summary of how the psalmist has blessedly received forgiveness.

- The description of troubles is a depiction of the physical strain of guilt.

- There's a characteristic recollection of the cry for help.

- The psalmist praises God for his deliverance.

- The psalmist then turns to address those who've come for the celebration meal and encourages them to learn the lessons of this experience.
- Finally, there's a call to join in praise and worship.

Reading the penitential psalms shouldn't lead to a morbid, paralyzing introspection whereby we repeatedly search every crevice of our lives for any scrap of sin we might not have yet identified. These psalmists are only too aware of their own sin. "I know my transgressions, and my sin is always before me," the writer of Psalm 51 says. "Day and night your hand was heavy on me," says the author of Psalm 32. They're guilty, and they know it.

⮑ If you're guilty, and you know it, take encouragement from these psalms to confess your sins to God and experience the blessedness of forgiveness. But do this discreetly. You don't need to reveal all the details of your sin to everyone in your group or church. Speak privately to God, and perhaps with one or two close friends or a trusted spiritual advisor. You may need to set the record straight or make restitution, but you can do even these things publicly without exposing a lot of unnecessary details. (Note that while there's a tradition that David wrote Psalm 51 after committing adultery, these psalms themselves give no details about the authors' actual sins.) If you need to go off by yourself or with one or two friends to pray right now, that's fine. You can use these psalms to help put your own experience into words. Your group will support you in prayer and welcome you back to this meeting, or to its next one, if you need to use all of your time now for prayer, confession, and restitution.

⮑ It is appropriate to declare publicly how blessed it is to be forgiven. Based on times when you've been forgiven yourself and also on these psalmists' descriptions of guilt and forgiveness, what words would you use to describe what it feels like to be forgiven? (For example, "free," "light," "refreshed," etc.) Again without revealing unnecessary details, explain why you'd use these particular words.

3 Psalm 51 appeals only to God's "unfailing love" and "great compassion" as reasons why he should forgive. But other penitential psalms, such as Psalms 39 and 90, cite another reason: life passes so quickly, and it's already filled with so much sorrow and trouble, that if God kept punishing people for their sins, life would hardly be worth living. So the psalmists plead for mercy, and ask God to keep them aware of the brevity of life so they can live wisely and well. (In session 8, we saw a similar argument in Psalm 102.) Have different people read Psalms 39 and 90 aloud for the group.

The effect of sin here isn't crushing guilt or shame; it's a wasted life. These psalmists aren't overwhelmed by the weight of conscience, but rather struck by how quickly life is passing without any real joy or meaning. Recognizing and admitting that we're not properly valuing our brief days on earth is a form of confession; the reorientation that comes from resolving to live for what is truly meaningful is genuine repentance.

➲ Identify the places in Psalms 39 and 90 where the writers ask God to show them how short their lives are. Would you like God to do this for you? Why or why not?

➲ If you were granted a respite from some of the more pressing troubles of life, in what meaningful way would you like to use the time and energy this would give you? What would God need to do for you so that you could use more of your time and energy this way now? Pray together as a group that God would do these needed things in the lives of each of your members.

FOR FURTHER READING AND DISCUSSION

- Psalm 25 is an individual penitential psalm. It begins with a statement of trust and includes a petition for deliverance from enemies, but its main theme is confession of sin and prayer for forgiveness, including the request, "Do not remember the sins of my youth and my rebellious ways." If you now look back over your life and regret things that you did in the immaturity or impetuousness of youth, use this psalm to help express your own prayer for forgiveness.

- Psalm 85 is a penitential psalm spoken, like Psalm 90, on behalf of the community. Like Psalm 40, it begins as a thanksgiving and becomes a supplication. Make this psalm the basis of your own prayer for a community that you're part of.

- Psalm 79 is another community penitential psalm, written in response to the destruction of Jerusalem. Read this psalm and note how it interweaves complaint, imprecation, confession of sin, and petition. You'll learn more about the destruction of Jerusalem and see further responses to it in session 19.

PSALMS OF PRAISE THAT CELEBRATE GOD'S REIGN and SONGS OF ZION

Divine Enthronement Psalms

INTRODUCTION

Just as particular elements of a psalm of supplication can be expanded to create compositions of a distinct character (psalms of trust, imprecatory psalms, etc.), so new forms can result when the elements of a psalm of praise are expanded. In session 6 we considered Psalms 148 and 150 and saw that the *call to worship* can be expanded so that it makes up most or all of a psalm. The same thing can happen with the *reason to worship*.

We've seen in earlier sessions that God's power and goodness can be questioned in a psalm of supplication, vindicated in a psalm of thanksgiving, and celebrated in a psalm of praise. Some praise psalms celebrate the way God is enthroned as King above all the earth, so that from that position of authority he can exercise his power on behalf of justice and show his goodness to the needy. The theme of God's enthronement can characterize a whole psalm of praise, and the description of it as a reason to worship can expand to fill an entire psalm. Songs like these are known as **divine enthronement psalms**. They embody the characteristic stance of psalms of praise: God is on the throne of heaven and all's right with the world, or all will be made right as God's reign is extended.

READING AND DISCUSSION

1 Have someone read Psalm 47 for the group. Notice that it's a two-part psalm of praise with two calls to worship, each one followed by a reason to worship introduced by "for."

Both parts of this psalm depict God as the supreme King. In this time kings would lead armies in battle, so God is described as a victorious warrior ("he subdued nations under us"). The psalm also describes God's actual enthronement, alluding to the celebrations at a coronation ceremony: "God has ascended [to the throne] amid shouts of joy, the LORD amid the sounding of trumpets."

⊃ What images would communicate to your culture that God is the supreme ruler of the world?

⊃ Psalm 47 is traditionally read at celebrations of Rosh Hashanah, the Jewish New Year, as a way of acknowledging God's rule over the year ahead. What would it be like for you to use Psalm 47 at the beginning of a calendar year or an academic year, on a significant anniversary, or at the start of an important enterprise to submit the days ahead to God's authority?

2 Have someone read Psalm 93. Note that the reason for praise, the declaration of God's enthronement, makes up this entire psalm.

God's power is described as "mightier than the thunder of the great waters." This is at least imagery describing God's power as greater than one of the loudest sounds anyone in this culture would ever hear. But in Hebrew thought the waters of the sea were a symbol of primordial chaos, so this may also be a declaration that God has defeated this enemy and created stability: "The world is established, firm and secure." At the end of the psalm God is praised for his just laws, which create stability within human society: "Your statutes, LORD, stand firm."

⊃ What symbolism or imagery would you use to depict the forces of chaos in the world? How would you envision God defeating them?

⊃ Describe a way in which you believe you've seen God establish justice and restore stability to human society, either in history or in your own personal experience.

3 One variation on the divine enthronement psalm celebrates the *place* of God's rule as a means of asserting the *fact* of God's rule. Psalms like this offer lyrical descriptions of the city of Jerusalem as a place of divine royal abode. They often call this city Zion, after the mountain it stands on, and so these psalms are known as **songs of Zion**. Have someone read Psalm 48 for the group. Note that it, too, gives reasons to worship without any formal call to worship.

This psalm has the same themes as Psalms 47 and 93. It celebrates God's kingship by depicting him as a victorious warrior (in this case, he has turned back an attack from the sea, scattering the invading ships) and as a righteous judge. But this depiction rests largely on a description of God's royal capital, Jerusalem, as the "city of the Great King." Mount Zion is said to be "like the heights of Zaphon," the mythic mountain at the far north of the world where Canaanite deities supposedly lived. (See NIV note.) The Lord's authority is said to extend from this superlative symbolic location, something like Mount Everest at the North Pole, "to the ends of the earth" and to last "for ever and ever."

⊃ In your culture, what locations are associated with power and authority? If they're natural locations, what are their defining features? If they were built by people, why were they situated where they are? Use these locations as figures of speech to describe God's reign over the world.

⊃ If you wish, conclude your time together by listening to the 1970s classic rock version of Psalm 93 by The Second Chapter of Acts, from their album *Mansion Builder*. (Note: Matthew Ward was 19 years old when he wrote and recorded this song. Offer your encouragement to any teenagers in your community who are trying to write their own songs.)

FOR FURTHER READING AND DISCUSSION

Read and discuss the following divine enthronement psalms and songs of Zion:

- Psalm 29 describes God as "enthroned over the flood . . . as King forever." By conquering the watery chaos, God has demonstrated his victorious power. His might is also symbolized by the loud sounds of thunder and breaking waves. (The song "The Earth Is Yours" by the group Gungor is based on Psalm 29.)

- Psalm 76 depicts God as a victorious warrior to describe how he is the supreme ruler who is "feared by the kings of the earth" and who "saves all the afflicted of the land." This psalm includes a four-part reference to the place of God's rule.

- Psalm 87 is a song of Zion that inspired John Newton's hymn "Glorious Things of Thee Are Spoken." The psalm describes people who belong to God as those who were "born in Zion." Newton drew on this image to describe followers of Jesus as "members of Zion's city." What does this idea mean to you?

- Psalm 68 insists that Mount Zion is more glorious than the "majestic" and "rugged" Mount Bashan because Zion is "the mountain where God chooses to reign." This psalm uses a theophany to depict God as a victorious warrior. It then describes a worship procession to the temple in Jerusalem.

PSALMS OF PRAISE THAT CELEBRATE GOD'S CARE FOR CREATION

INTRODUCTION

Psalms of praise may celebrate one particular aspect of God's power or goodness, in an extended reason-to-worship section. In this session we'll look at psalms that describe the way God shows his goodness by caring for the created world.

READING AND DISCUSSION

1 Psalm 104 is a psalm of praise that begins much like a divine enthronement psalm. It describes how the Lord is "clothed with splendor and majesty" and how he has "set the earth on its foundations" so that "it can never be moved." Like Psalm 93, this psalm also celebrates God's victory over the watery forces of chaos. But it offers a more extended depiction of how God (in his original acts of creation or at the end of the great flood) drew the dry land out from the waters. In the ancient view of the universe, the sky ("the heavens") was a solid dome above the earth and sea, and there were waters above the sky itself, so God could live in "upper chambers" supported on beams above these waters.

The main message of Psalm 104 is that from this exalted position, God sends down rain and ensures that the waters on earth remain in their proper channels so that they provide drink for the thirsty and irrigate the land so it brings forth crops. The psalm offers a meditation on how all living things—beasts of the field, birds of the sky, creatures of the sea, and human beings—look to God for their food. It depicts creatures thriving in their own proper habitats: wild goats on high mountains, storks in juniper trees, aquatic life "frolicking" in the ocean, etc. There is a circle of life in which some creatures die and new ones take their place, but the overall picture is of God watering the earth and continually renewing the "face of the ground."

Have someone read Psalm 104 out loud. Notice that it begins and ends with brief calls to worship, but consists almost entirely of an extended reason to worship.

⮑ Psalm 104 represents God not just as the original Creator of the world, but as someone who actively and continually sustains natural life. This isn't something that can be demonstrated scientifically. But if you believe by faith that God is doing this, how does this shape the way you relate to the natural world yourself?

⮑ Even though God has "set a boundary" that the waters "cannot cross," floods, hurricane storm surges, and tsunamis still take place. But these are exceptions to a regular pattern of tides, river flow, and roughly predictable rainfall that, as the psalm says, permits human culture to flourish through agriculture and navigation. Go around the room and give each person a chance to ask God a question out loud that they have about destruction that's been caused by raging waters. Then go around again and give each person the chance to thank God for something good that dependable waters have made possible.

⮑ As Psalm 104 illustrates, a supply of good water is vital for life and flourishing. In many parts of the world, people spend much of their time and labor simply going to get water. What organizations do you know that are working to provide people with clean water in their own communities? Have you been to see any of their work? What could your group do to support one of these organizations?

2 Psalm 65 begins more like a psalm of thanksgiving than a psalm of praise. It depicts a vow being paid and a celebration meal being held in the temple, and it recounts how God has forgiven the people's sins and rescued them from some threat, which is symbolized by God's victory over the watery forces of chaos ("the roaring of the seas"). But the psalm then turns to praise God for his ongoing care of creation. Like Psalm 104 it describes how God waters the earth so that it brings forth an abundant harvest. The psalm concludes with a beautiful image of the landscape being clothed with flocks and grain. The hills and valleys themselves provide the closing note of praise as they "shout for joy and sing." Have someone read Psalm 65 for the group.

➲ Find out who in the group has a garden, and what they grow in it. Who has worked on a farm or in a similar enterprise such as a winery, mushroom cellar, dairy, etc.? Have you ever seen a "bumper crop" that seemed to "clothe" the garden or farm?

➲ If God has "ordained" to "provide the people with grain," why are so many people still hungry today? What can followers of Jesus do to overcome hunger in their own communities and around the world?

3 Psalm 8 is a psalm of praise that begins and ends not with a call to worship but with an expression of worship: "Lord, our Lord, how majestic is your name in all the earth!" In between, as a reason to worship, the psalm surveys all of creation, starting in the heavens with the moon and stars and angels, then moving down to human beings, and finally to animals, birds, and sea creatures. It exclaims how remarkable it is that God should entrust people, who are so insignificant in the grand scheme of things, with the vital role of being "rulers" over the earth. This assigned role doesn't mean that people have the right to exploit or pillage the creation. Rather, they are its caretakers and stewards, on God's behalf. One very important way that God wants to care for his own creation is through people. Have someone read Psalm 8.

➲ Give everyone the chance to share the top three ways they've been able to care for creation in their current life situation. Can "going green" be a way of expressing faith in God and accepting a responsibility to be the kind of "ruler" that God intended?

PSALMS OF PRAISE THAT CELEBRATE GOD'S COMPASSION

INTRODUCTION

Another aspect of God's goodness that biblical psalms of praise celebrate is the compassion he shows to those in need. This may be described in an extended reason-to-worship section that makes up most of a psalm.

READING AND DISCUSSION

1 Psalm 113 is an elegantly balanced psalm of praise. It begins and ends with the call *Hallelu Yah*. In between, it has three stanzas of three lines each. The first stanza is a call to worship, a summons for people to praise God's name all through time and space. The second stanza, just like a divine enthronement psalm, cites God's exaltation "over all the nations" and "above the heavens" as a reason for worship. The third stanza, as a further reason for worship, celebrates how God has compassion on the poor and needy.

Have three different people read the three stanzas of this psalm, with the whole group reading "Praise the LORD" together at the beginning and end.

➲ This psalm says the poor and needy are in the "dust"— homeless, living and sleeping on the ground. They stay near the "ash heap," the garbage dump where ashes are tossed from cooking fires. There they can at least stay warm, and perhaps find some charcoal to use or sell. The psalm envisions God feeding, clothing, and housing them, and raising them to places of influence and leadership in the community. Do you know anyone who is, or has been, homeless? Do you know of, or have you visited, any communities that have grown up around garbage dumps? Tell the group about any organizations you know that are effectively helping people move out of homelessness and poverty.

⮑ This psalm depicts God's acts of compassion as a vital expression and extension of his reign. Do you associate the works of compassion that followers of Jesus do today with the coming reign or kingdom of God? Why or why not?

2 Have someone read Psalm 146. Notice that it's a chiasm:

> *Hallelu Yah*
>> Statement of praise
>>> Reasons not to trust in human beings
>>> Reasons to hope in the LORD
>> Statement of the LORD's reign
> *Hallelu Yah*

The bulk of this psalm is an extended reason-to-worship section that praises God first as the Creator, and then at length as the compassionate provider for all those in need. The concluding declaration of the LORD's reign identifies this compassion as an expression of his divine rule.

⮑ Divide your group into teams of two or three people and assign each of these terms in Psalm 146 to a team: the oppressed, the hungry, prisoners, the blind, those who are bowed down, the righteous, the foreigner, the fatherless, the widow. Have each team imagine what life was like in biblical times for these people. Why did they need God's help? What does Psalm 146 describe God doing for them? Who corresponds to these people today? What can followers of Jesus do to help them? Each team should report its conclusions back to the whole group.

3 Psalm 145 is a special kind of composition. It has 22 lines that begin with the 22 letters of the Hebrew alphabet in consecutive order. This kind of composition is known as an **acrostic**. A couple of psalms you've already considered, Psalms 9–10 and 25, are also acrostics, and you'll encounter more of them in later sessions. The alphabetic pattern may be used as an aid to memory, and also to depict a composition as speaking comprehensively about a subject. Here it helps portray God's reign as total and comprehensive, just as Psalm 113 describes it extending through all of space and time.

There's often a significant statement or transition in the middle of an acrostic that divides it into two parts. This is true of Psalm 145. Its first part describes God being praised; his compassion is mentioned briefly as one reason for praise. In the center of the psalm, the writer speaks three times about God's kingdom. This is a thematic statement that constitutes a transition. Then, in the second part, God's compassionate character is described in more detail.

⮑ Psalm 145 describes God as gracious, compassionate, trustworthy, and faithful. What does each of these terms mean? As a group, work together to define and illustrate them. If God's character is perfect and complete, and his reign is total and limitless, then God's exercise of these qualities is never flawed or partial, and he will never run out of the goodness that generates them. God never gets "compassion fatigue." Describe for yourself, and for the group if it's appropriate to do so, the situation in which you most need a fresh supply of God's pure, unending compassion for others in need. Pray for one another, that you will each receive this supply.

PSALMS OF PRAISE THAT CELEBRATE GOD'S JUSTICE

INTRODUCTION

In this session we'll look at psalms that celebrate the way God uses his exalted position of authority to ensure justice throughout the world. The theme of God as a righteous judge was one part of the portrayal of his kingly power and goodness in the divine enthronement psalms we looked at in session 12, but it's the main focus of the ones we'll consider here.

READING AND DISCUSSION

1 Psalm 99 begins by declaring the fact of God's enthronement and describing how he has used his kingly power to establish justice on earth generally. Then it explains that God specifically used "the statutes and the decrees" that he gave to Moses and Aaron in the law, which prophets like Samuel upheld, to create justice within Israel.

This is a song with two stanzas, followed by a repeated chorus. Each stanza first speaks about God, then to God. The chorus is a call to worship that follows these reasons to worship. Read the psalm like this:

- Have one person read the first part of each stanza, which speaks about God.

- Have the others respond by reading the next part of each stanza, which is addressed to God (starting "The King is mighty" and "Lord our God, you answered them").
- Have everyone read the choruses together ("Exalt the Lord our God and worship at his footstool/holy mountain; he is holy").

Many interpreters believe that this psalm was sung responsively like this in the temple.

➲ Psalm 99 uses three different terms to describe what God's rule brings about on earth. While there's considerable overlap between them, each one has a particular focus. "Justice" often refers to deciding between the competing interests of contending parties in a way that's fair to each of them. "Equity" describes a person who always applies the same straightforward principles, no matter who they're dealing with. "Righteousness" is the quality of someone who does the right thing as an expression of their inner character. To illustrate God's nature as ruler of the world, what examples can you give of different people who've exemplified one of these terms on particular occasions?

2 Have someone read Psalm 97. Notice that it's a chiasm:

> Call to worship the Lord (addressed to creation)
> > Reason to worship the Lord
> > > Call not to worship any other "gods"
> > Reason to worship the Lord
> Call to worship the Lord (addressed to people)

The first reason to worship depicts God's power in a theophany, using the imagery of a thunderstorm. Here God's justice is tied directly to the exercise of his kingly power: "Clouds and thick darkness surround him; righteousness and justice are the foundation of his throne." The second reason to worship is God's "judgments" themselves: "He guards the lives of his faithful ones and delivers them from the hand of the wicked." In between, the psalm says that all who worship any other so-called gods are "put to shame." These "gods" have no power, and they don't uphold justice. In fact, the psalm calls on them, such as they may be, to surrender their claims and acknowledge that the LORD is the supreme God. It also calls on those who "love the LORD" to "hate evil" and practice righteousness as the true expression of their worship and devotion to the just ruler of the world.

⮑ If you are a follower of Jesus, how have you joined in God's work of establishing justice on earth, as an expression of the way you worship and serve the true God rather than a false god?

3 In the ancient world kings were also the supreme judges in their lands. So when Psalm 82 proclaims, "God presides in the great assembly; he renders judgment among the 'gods,'" this is another way of describing God's enthronement as King over all. This psalm pictures God gathering together all the so-called "gods" of the other nations and rebuking them for not upholding justice in the lands where they're worshipped. Because they "know nothing" and aren't maintaining justice, "all the foundations of the earth are shaken." So this psalm pictures God dismissing all these "gods" as no more powerful or divine than "mere mortals." The psalmist then concludes by calling on God to "judge the earth," since he is actually the rightful ruler of "all the nations." Have someone read Psalm 82 for the group.

⮑ What false "gods" are "worshipped" where you live? That is, what things are believed to be capable of granting authentic life to people? (For example, wealth, education, beauty, power, entertainment, sports, technology, formal religion, the family, the nation, etc.) Convene a "great assembly" and pass judgment on these "gods" for their failure to deliver true justice in the spheres where they're worshipped. You can have some group members take on their parts and try to justify themselves, while others can form a tribunal that judges them on behalf of God, using the standards described in Psalm 82.

⮑ If you wish, conclude your time together by singing Cindy Rethmeier's song "Exalt the LORD," which is based on the chorus of

Psalm 99, or by listening to or watching the version of this song by the group Six Steps.

FOR FURTHER READING AND DISCUSSION

- Psalm 75, like Psalm 82, describes God as the supreme ruler whose justice holds the world together: "When the earth and all its people quake, it is I who hold its pillars firm." Read this psalm and notice its elements, images, and themes. What is its primary message?
- Read Psalm 67. Note how it combines the justice emphasis of the psalms you considered in this session with the harvest emphasis you saw in Psalm 65 (session 13) as complementary expressions of God's rule.

WISDOM PSALMS

INTRODUCTION

Many psalms make a practical application of the truth about God's justice. They teach their listeners about the two very different fates that await the wicked and the righteous, and they urge them to cultivate wisdom, the ability to choose the right path in life, by fearing the LORD.

Some of these wisdom psalms look quite different from the types we've considered so far. They're spoken to other people, rather than to God, and they're essentially teaching rather than supplication, thanksgiving, or praise. But other wisdom psalms present their teaching within the framework of one of the basic types.

In this session we'll first consider a teaching-type wisdom psalm, to appreciate its distinctive form and message. Then we'll consider three psalms that are based on the supplication, thanksgiving, and praise forms, but which have been transformed to become vehicles for wisdom. Finally, we'll look at another teaching-type wisdom psalm.

READING AND DISCUSSION

1 Have someone read Psalm 37 for the group. As you listen, notice how it's different from the other types of psalms you've encountered so far. (It's spoken to people and emphasizes teaching.)

One basic message runs all the way through Psalm 37: the wicked may succeed and prosper for a time, but they will inevitably be destroyed by their own wickedness. So don't be afraid of them, and don't be tempted to imitate them! Instead, patiently persevere in doing what's right, and you'll be blessed over the long term. This is the essence of the wisdom teaching of the ancient world, which is captured within the Bible in books like Proverbs and in psalms like this one.

Psalm 37 is an acrostic. In this case, every second line begins with the next letter of the Hebrew alphabet, so the psalm has 44 lines in all. The alphabetic pattern, as we noted in session 14, is likely an aid to memory, and it also signifies here how wisdom provides a comprehensive understanding of life.

⮑ Divide your group into three teams and have each team go back through Psalm 37 and investigate one of these questions and report its findings to the group:
- According to this psalm, how do the righteous live differently from the wicked?
- What specific things does this psalm encourage people to do in their relationship with the Lord?
- What promises does the psalm make to the righteous? (What will God do for them?)

⮑ After the teams report back, give each person a chance to share one way in which they've been challenged to live or to relate to God differently in order to follow the path of wisdom, or one thing they're hoping to experience if they do.

2 Psalm 94 is a *psalm of supplication* that has been transformed to become a vehicle for wisdom teaching. It begins characteristically with a cry for help, followed by a complaint about how the wicked are violently oppressing the weak. It includes a petition ("Who will rise up for me against the wicked?") and a statement of trust, expressing confidence in the Lord. All of these elements are addressed to God. But the psalm also addresses human listeners, urging all those who think "the Lord does not see" to get greater wisdom: "You fools, when will you become wise?" Like other wisdom psalms, it explains how God punishes the wicked but protects and blesses the righteous. In an artful twist on the basic supplication form, Psalm 94 ends with a promise of payment, but not of a vow the psalmist has made. Instead, it says God will "repay" the wicked for what they have done.

In wisdom teaching, the term "fool" doesn't refer to someone who lacks intelligence or education. Rather, it refers to anyone who lives as if God didn't exist or as if God couldn't do anything about injustice on earth. The fool recklessly does wrong, fearing no consequences. The basic message of Psalm 94 is, there will be consequences.

> ➲ Can you remember a time when you discovered that there are consequences for the reckless or heedless choices people make in life? Without revealing unnecessary details, share with the group something of what you experienced or observed, if you can.

3 Psalm 34 is a *psalm of thanksgiving* that has been transformed to become a vehicle for wisdom teaching. It begins in the standard way, with a call to worship and a summary of the psalmist's experience that includes a recollection of the cry for help. The psalm invites the listeners to share in a celebratory meal: "Taste and see that the Lord is good; blessed is the one who takes refuge in him." But the gathering of family and friends then provides an occasion for the psalmist to teach the lessons of this deliverance to the next generation: "Come, my children, listen to me; I will teach you the fear of the Lord."

The singer then actually poses a question. We can picture the children eagerly raising their hands in response: "Who here wants to have a great life, and see good things happen all through it?" ("I do! I do!") Then if that's the case, the psalmist continues, you need to "turn from evil and do good." The rest of the psalm instructively contrasts God's favor towards the righteous with God's judgment of the wicked.

Psalm 34 is another acrostic, with each of its 22 poetic lines beginning with the letters of the Hebrew alphabet in consecutive order. This type of composition is a favorite of wisdom teachers; it's also used at the end of Proverbs.

⮑ What lessons of experience would you most like to pass on to younger friends and family members? Are there statements in any of these wisdom psalms that help you summarize these lessons?

4 Psalm 112 is a *psalm of praise* that has been transformed to become a vehicle for wisdom teaching. It retains only a hint of the basic form, beginning with a brief call to worship. The teaching it presents is then like an extended reason to worship, celebrating God's justice. However, it speaks about the contrast between the fates of the righteous and the wicked without specifying that it's the LORD, enthroned in the heavens, whose reign of justice is reflected in these fates. This psalm presents the same overall message as Psalm 37, but with a greater emphasis on the long-term prosperity of the righteous and only a closing note about the futility of wickedness.

Psalm 112 is also an acrostic, but in this case, its half-lines begin with the consecutive letters of the alphabet, so that the psalm as a whole has only 11 lines. They're built out of 22 brief phrases, mostly of 3 or 4 words each. (Hebrew poetry is very compact in its expression.) This simplicity suggests that the writer may have intended for children to memorize this psalm.

⮑ See if, as a group, you can compose an acrostic wisdom psalm using the letters of your own alphabet at the start of brief statements that contrast the righteous with the wicked, as in Psalms 37 and 112. (For example, "**A**lways fear the LORD. **B**lessings come that way." And so forth.)

⮑ See if you can memorize Psalm 112 and recite it for your group at its next meeting.

5 Psalm 49 is another teaching-type wisdom psalm. It develops the same basic theme as Psalm 37: even if the wicked prosper and become rich, don't be afraid of them and don't envy them, because they're destined to lose all of their ill-gotten gains. But instead of saying that God will destroy the wicked when the "day" for their judgment arrives, this psalm offers the complementary observation that no one can take their riches with them when they die. And so the true way of wisdom is to live as one of the upright, whom God will "redeem . . . from the realm of the dead" and "take . . . to himself" forever.

Psalm 49 begins with an opening appeal for its listeners to pay attention to its "words of wisdom." The psalm says it will be presenting a *mashal* (NIV "proverb"), literally a comparison, which is drawn explicitly in the middle ("People, despite their wealth, do not endure; they *are like* the beasts that perish") and at the end ("People who have wealth but lack understanding *are like* the beasts that perish"). The psalm as a whole is designed, in classic wisdom style, to startle complacent listeners out of their uncritical admiration for the rich through a vivid comparison, describing how they are, in the end, no more immortal than the beasts.

⮑ How much money do you need to live a good life? How much is enough, and how much is too much? What would you like to do with some of your time and energy if you didn't have to spend all of it working for money?

⮑ Who would you like to inherit your money when you die? What measures have you taken to try to make sure they receive it? Is giving your money away while you're still alive the only certain way to know where it's going to go?

FOR FURTHER READING AND DISCUSSION

- Read Psalms 36, 73, 92, and 111, and note their wisdom themes. (Psalm 111 is an acrostic by half-line, like Psalm 112.) Which of the basic forms do each of these psalms most resemble (supplication, thanksgiving, praise)? Which of their statements are reminiscent of the other psalms you considered in this session?

- Psalm 14 is a wisdom psalm that most often uses the name *Yahweh* ("the Lord") to speak about God. Psalm 53 is a later adaptation of it, almost identical in wording, that instead uses the name *Elohim* ("God") throughout. It's not entirely clear why this second version was created. Consider the psalm in either version and note how it provides a classic definition and description of the "fool" who lives without regard for God.

To find more about biblical wisdom literature, see the study guide to Proverbs, Ecclesiastes, and James in the Understanding the Books of the Bible series.

PSALMS OF THE LAW

INTRODUCTION

Some wisdom psalms describe the principles and commandments found in the law of Moses as a vital source of training and enlightenment for anyone who wants to become wise. Psalm 37 says, "The mouths of the righteous utter wisdom, and their tongues speak what is just. The law of their God is in their hearts; their feet do not slip." Psalm 94 says similarly, "Blessed is the one you discipline, LORD, the one you teach from your law." Certain psalms focus more directly on the benefits of carefully studying and reflecting on God's principles and commandments. These are known as **psalms of the law**.

READING AND DISCUSSION

1 Have someone read Psalm 1 for the group. This psalm describes delighting in and meditating on the law of the LORD as the safeguard against a futile and precarious life. Like other wisdom psalms, it contrasts the steady productivity and lasting achievements of the righteous with the inevitable destruction of the wicked.

⮑ Psalm 1 describes an incautious person getting inexorably drawn in by the wicked: first walking along with them, then stopping to stand with them, and finally settling right down in their midst. Give an illustration of how taking the first steps down an unwise path can escalate into serious wrongdoing under the influence of bad company. Then cite some biblical principles that would keep a person from going down that path in the first place.

⮑ For followers of Jesus today, the completed Bible represents what the law of Moses did for this psalmist. What does it look like to "delight" in the Scriptures? Do you know someone who does this (or did when they were alive)? Describe their attitude and feelings towards the Bible and how they engage or engaged it.

⮑ In this culture most people weren't literate, and copies of the Scriptures weren't widely available. In order to build God's Word into their lives, people would have to *remember* what they heard from it in the temple or synagogue, or in a conversation with a teacher, and *reflect* on its meaning and implications. This is what Psalm 1 means when it speaks of "meditating" on the Scriptures: remembering and reflecting. What are some good ways to do this today? How are people both better off and worse off in situations where almost everyone can read and where copies of the Bible are widely available?

2 Have someone read Psalm 19 for the group. This psalm describes two sources of knowledge about God: nature and Scripture. It first portrays how the created world wordlessly but eloquently proclaims the glory of its Maker. It then describes the virtues of God's Word, describing it by a variety of synonyms and recounting its benefits. The psalm concludes with a petition for discernment, forgiveness, and restraint and with a prayer for words and thoughts that are pleasing to God.

➲ Which of the following benefits listed in this psalm have you experienced from your own engagement with Scripture? Tell your group how.

- refreshment of the soul
- wisdom for the simple
- joy to the heart
- light to the eyes
- warning
- great reward

➲ Which of the following statements best expresses your understanding of the relationship between the natural world and the Scriptures as sources of truth about God?

a. The Bible is a description of the world from God's omniscient perspective, so any observations people make that seem to contradict Scripture must be wrong.

b. Contemporary scientific tools and techniques permit much more accurate observations than were possible in biblical times, so any apparent contradictions have to be resolved in favor of science.

c. Science and Scripture are complementary sources of information about God. Each one has its proper sphere and neither should try to answer questions that the other is best qualified to address.

3 Psalm 119 is a heartfelt and extended prayer for understanding of the Scriptures. It repeatedly asks God to "teach" his ways so the psalmist can find the right path in life and escape from threats and danger. As in the center section of Psalm 19, each poetic line uses one of a variety of synonyms to speak about the Scriptures: as God's law, statutes, ways, precepts, decrees, commands, word, etc. This psalm is an acrostic in which eight lines in a row begin with each letter of the Hebrew alphabet, so it has 8 x 22 or 176 lines in all. The alphabetic pattern is once again probably intended as an aid to memory. (Simply hearing the value of the Scriptures described 176 different ways would make a lasting impression. Think how deeply the message would be impressed on anyone who memorized this psalm!)

Read through Psalm 119 together as a group. This should take less than ten minutes. Take turns reading an eight-line section each. (In *The Books of the Bible*, these sections are marked off by a little extra white space. Many other editions use the names or symbols of the Hebrew letters to mark them off, for example, "א Aleph" or just "Aleph.") When it's your turn to read, speak the words as a prayer, and use them to express your own heartfelt desire to understand the Scriptures better and benefit from their teaching. As you're reading and listening, notice the different ways in which the Scriptures are described. Also notice what words and phrases are repeated throughout the psalm. If a particular statement speaks to you, make a note of it.

⮑ What repeated words and phrases did you notice in Psalm 119? How do they help emphasize its overall meaning? What particular statements in the psalm spoke to you personally? Why?

⮑ Why does the psalmist ask so often for God to actively "teach" his law? Isn't it enough just to read the Bible and learn from it that way?

⮑ What songs or hymns do you know that describe the value of understanding and following God's Word? (For example, Isaac Watts' hymn "The Heavens Declare Thy Glory, Lord," based on Psalm 19; Amy Grant's song "Thy Word is a Lamp Unto My Feet," based on a line from Psalm 119; or even the children's song "The B-I-B-L-E.") Sing one of these songs together if you wish.

SALVATION HISTORY PSALMS

INTRODUCTION

We noted in the previous session that while most people were not literate in ancient Israel and copies of the Scriptures were rare, people could still learn about the Scriptures in the temple or synagogue and also find out about them from teachers. One more way ancient Israelites could hear the story told in the Scriptures was through certain of the psalms. Some longer psalms recount the story of Israel's relationship with God down through the centuries. They're known as **salvation history psalms**.

This name describes their *content*, not their *form*. What salvation history psalms all have in common is the way they tell Israel's story at some length. But in form, they may be psalms of praise, wisdom psalms, psalms of supplication, or penitential psalms, as we'll see in this session.

READING AND DISCUSSION

1 Psalm 105 is a psalm of praise that begins with a call to worship and ends with another brief call to worship (*Hallelu Yah*). In between, in an extended reason to worship, God is acknowledged as the one whose "judgments are in all the earth." In this case God is not as much being celebrated as the righteous judge of the world, as he was in the psalms of praise we considered in session 15. Rather, he's being honored as the Lord of history, who steadily works out his redemptive plan through the affairs of the nations. Specifically, this psalm recounts salvation history to acknowledge God for the way he fulfilled his covenant promises to Abraham and his descendants.

In its opening, this psalm calls on its listeners to "meditate on" (NIV "tell of") God's wonderful acts. This is the same verb that's used five times in Psalm 119 in regard to the Scriptures (for example, "Cause me to understand the way of your precepts, that I may *meditate* on your wonderful deeds"). This verb is also a synonym of the word for "meditate" in Psalm 1. The implication is that it's just as important and valuable to know, retell, and reflect on the big story of God's dealings with humanity as it is to do this with individual passages of Scripture.

⊃ How well would you say you know the "big story" of God? What are some good ways to get to know this story better? (As you listened to Psalm 105, did you recognize the various episodes it relates? See if, as a group, you can identify where these episodes come and how they relate to each other in the big story that unfolds in the Bible.) Do you recognize your own place within the unfolding story of God? How does this help you see significance and direction in your own life? (You can explore these topics further at www.Biblica.com/LivingtheScript.)

2 Psalm 78 is a wisdom psalm, much like Psalm 49. It begins by calling on people to hear its teaching, and it says it's going to present a *mashal* (NIV "parable"), a comparison. In this case the comparison is between the Israelites in the wilderness, who "did not remember [God's] power, the day he redeemed them from the oppressor," and the armies of the tribe of Ephraim, who at some later point also failed to trust God and "turned back" because they "forgot what he had done, the wonders he had shown them." In both cases, the psalm says, what the people should have remembered was how God delivered Israel from slavery in Egypt. Instead, they questioned and disobeyed God, and when God "heard them, he was furious." This is why, the psalm explains, God chose David from the tribe of Judah to lead Israel, rather than the large, powerful, centrally located tribe of Ephraim. Have someone read Psalm 78.

The message of this psalm for its original audience is that everyone in Israel, particularly in the tribe of Ephraim, should understand and accept God's reasons for choosing David and not wish for a different royal house from a tribe such as their own. The wider implications, for all places and times, are that the "praiseworthy deeds of the Lord" should be recounted from generation to generation, so that people will "put their trust in God" and "not forget his deeds."

⊃ Looking back over your own life, do you feel that you've ever turned back from trusting God because you forgot the things he'd done for you? Do you think this made God frustrated . . . upset . . . angry . . . furious?

⊃ What should you have remembered? Which of the things that God has done in your own life, and in history and the Scriptures, give you the greatest confidence in his power and goodness? What can you do to ensure that you remember these things and so trust God when you face difficult challenges, rather than forget them and question or disobey God?

⊃ Like Psalm 105, Psalm 78 looks back to the Exodus, God's deliverance of the Israelites from slavery in Egypt, as a foundational event that should give all later believers confidence that God can deliver them as well. (In session 2, we saw this process at work in Psalm 77.) Followers of Jesus live at a later time in the story of God when Jesus' death and resurrection are now the foundational event. How can the cross and the empty tomb give you confidence that you can depend on God? What songs do you know that, like salvation history psalms, call you back to these events?

FOR FURTHER READING AND DISCUSSION

Read and discuss these other salvation history psalms, which illustrate the variety of forms the retelling of Israel's story can take.

- Psalm 136 is a praise psalm that cites God's works in creation and in salvation history as reasons for worship. It has a call-and-response form, with a worship leader singing out what God has done and the people affirming each point by chanting together, "His love endures forever."

- Psalm 89 starts as a psalm of praise. It's mostly devoted to celebrating a particular quality of the divine character, the faithfulness that God promised to David and his descendants. But towards the end it abruptly turns into a psalm of supplication, complaining that God has "renounced the covenant" he made with David and "defiled his crown in the dust." It's referring to the conquest of Judah and the destruction of temple by the Babylonians, which we'll consider in more detail in the next session.

- Psalm 106 is a penitential psalm that asks God to forgive the many sins of the community and bring the people back from exile in Babylon ("gather us from the nations"). It retells the story of Israel up to the time of the destruction of Jerusalem and the exile. In each phase of the story, the emphasis is not so much on the wonders that God did, but rather on how the people continually disobeyed him. This extended confession ("we have sinned, even as our ancestors did; we have done wrong and acted wickedly") is offered in the hopes of receiving forgiveness and restoration. What would a penitential psalm look like that was written on behalf of your own nation, recounting its historic sins?

THE BOOK OF LAMENTATIONS

INTRODUCTION

As we saw last time, the Exodus, the deliverance from slavery in Egypt, was the foundational event of salvation history that gave ancient Israelites confidence in God's goodness and power. Many centuries later, another event occurred that shattered this confidence. When the Babylonians destroyed Jerusalem in 587 BC, the people were devastated. Their royal, religious, civic, and military leaders and institutions were all swept away. They had been warned repeatedly by prophets such as Jeremiah that this would happen if they didn't practice justice and compassion as God's laws required, but they ignored these warnings and suffered the horrible consequences.

It was a tremendous challenge to come to terms with this devastating event. Several of the psalms you've already considered represent attempts to do this. These include psalms of supplication, petitioning for mercy and restoration, such as Psalms 80 and 74 (sessions 1 and 2). They also include penitential psalms, composed on behalf of the community, acknowledging its sins and the justice of God's judgment, but also asking for mercy. These include Psalms 79 and 106 (sessions 11 and 18).

But the primary response in the Bible to the destruction of Jerusalem is in the book of Lamentations. As its title indicates, this is a collection of sorrowful, meditative songs that mourn this great tragedy. They are essentially psalms of supplication. While they contain many elements you're already familiar with such as confession of sin, petition for mercy, and imprecations against the wicked, their primary element is an extended expression of grief and sorrow.

There are five songs in the book of Lamentations. (Tradition associates them with the prophet Jeremiah, but we don't know for certain who wrote them.) The basic form of these songs is the acrostic, the alphabetical pattern you've seen already in several of the psalms. In this case, the acrostic form may be employed because the emotions these songs seek to convey are so powerful that they need an especially tight structure in order to be expressed.

However, there is variation within the acrostic pattern in Lamentations:

- The first, second, and third songs all have three-part lines; the fourth song has two-part lines; and the fifth song has one-part lines.

- In the first, second, and fourth songs, each full line begins with the appropriate letter of the alphabet. In the third song, all three parts of the line do. By contrast, in the fifth song, while there are still 22 lines suggesting the acrostic form, the lines don't follow any alphabetic pattern.

The overall impression, as the songs shorten and their form loosens, is of the singer's art and voice being lost and giving way to silence before the immensity of this tragedy.

READING

Have different people read the five songs in the book of Lamentations. This should take about 10 to 15 minutes. In *The Books of the Bible*, there's some extra white space between each song. (If you're using a different edition, you'll find that the traditional chapters correspond with the individual songs.) These songs describe the horrors of warfare and its aftermath, so choose people who are willing to read out loud some difficult material.

As you listen, notice how the city of Jerusalem often breaks in and speaks for herself, sometimes in extended passages, describing her devastation by saying "I" and "my." (For example, "Is any suffering like my suffering that was inflicted on me, that the LORD brought on me in the day of his fierce anger?")

Also notice the various elements you're familiar with from psalms of supplication as they occur: confessions of sin, imprecations against enemies, statements of trust, cries for help, and especially complaints (laments) that grieve over the city's ruin.

DISCUSSION

⊃ What is your response to hearing the book of Lamentations read out loud? (This is rarely done; should it be done more often? Why or why not?) What questions did this reading raise? What insights did it give you?

⊃ Have you ever seen a city that was largely destroyed by war or natural disaster? If so, tell the group what brought you there and something of your experience, to the extent that you can. How well do you feel Lamentations captures the experience of being in a ruined city? If you haven't had an experience like this personally, what situation did the book most bring to your mind? Why?

⊃ Throughout the book the conviction is expressed that Jerusalem was destroyed because it didn't practice the justice and compassion its covenant relationship with the LORD required. Because the city became so corrupted, God no longer defended it from its enemies, and they committed or caused all the atrocities that Lamentations details: massive destruction, murder, rape, starvation, even cannibalism. Because God abandoned the people to these things, would you say he is partly responsible for them? Why or why not? Is it consistent with divine justice for a whole city to suffer in these ways?

⮑ There are some hopeful passages in Lamentations, but they're in the middle. The book as a whole doesn't build up to a hopeful ending. Instead, it ends with a description of horrors and the question of whether God has "utterly rejected" Jerusalem because he is "angry . . . beyond measure." Why do you think this book of the Bible doesn't offer a more hopeful conclusion?

⮑ As we've noted, Jesus' death and resurrection are now the foundational events of salvation history that give his followers confidence in God's goodness and power. Have there been any events for followers of Jesus that are like the destruction of Jerusalem, which pose a great challenge to continuing belief in God's goodness and power?

FOR FURTHER READING AND DISCUSSION

- Look again at Psalm 79. How are its emphases similar to, and different from, those in the book of Lamentations?
- Read Psalm 74 once again. What more do you learn about the destruction of Jerusalem from this psalm? On what basis does the psalmist appeal to God to defend the people?
- In session 1 you read Psalm 80 as an illustration of the way psalms are songs. Reread this psalm now and see what more you understand, in light of the book of Lamentations, about the situation it was written to address.

PSALMS FOR SPECIAL OCCASIONS: CORONATION

INTRODUCTION

Some of the psalms were composed for special occasions. They reflect happier times in the life of the nation, before Jerusalem was destroyed and after the people returned from exile. These include coronation psalms, written to ask God's blessings on a newly crowned king.

READING AND DISCUSSION

1 Before the destruction of Jerusalem, kings in the line of David ruled from that city for several centuries. Psalm 72 is a prayer for a king who is just taking the throne. It asks God to give him a long reign over a broad territory; to let the people enjoy prosperity, peace, and justice throughout his days; and to make him a blessing to the nations all around. Have someone read Psalm 72 for the group.

⮑ Have you ever seen a coronation (the crowning of a king or queen), either in person or on television? If so, tell the group what this was like.

⮕ What hopes and expectations did you have the last time your country got a new president, prime minister, or other ruler that you really believed in? In what ways were you hoping this new leader would help bring greater peace, prosperity, and justice, both in your own country and around the world?

⮕ This is a psalm of supplication that consists entirely of an extended petition, except for three lines that offer a reason why God should grant these requests: the king will rescue the weak and needy from violence and oppression. Find these lines and read them again out loud. Why will this be the key to the success of this king's reign?

⮕ Do you pray regularly for your country's leader? As a group, use this psalm to pray that the leader of your country will be righteous, taking turns reading the lines and rewording them as appropriate. (For example, "Endow the president with your justice, O God, the chief executive with your righteousness.")

2 Psalm 101 is a series of vows that could have been composed by anyone in Israel who was choosing the way of the righteous rather than the way of the wicked. However, the psalm gives several indications that it was meant to be spoken by a king at the beginning of his reign. The speaker has the authority to punish "all the wicked in the land" and is responsible for a great "house" with many servants who must be honest and trustworthy. Many interpreters regard this psalm as a kind of "oath of office" that a new king of Israel would recite as a public pledge. Read Psalm 101 out loud in unison (all together).

⮕ What oath or pledge does a new leader of your country take? Find the exact words on the Internet, in an almanac, etc. How are they similar to, and different from, Psalm 101?

⊃ As noted, this psalm can appropriately be spoken by anyone who wants to choose the way of the righteous. (This is why you were all asked to read it together.) Who are some of the other influential people in your culture, besides political leaders, whom you'd like to see take a pledge like this? Would you take it publicly in your own sphere of influence?

⊃ Psalm 101 is like a psalm of praise. It begins with a declaration of worship in place of a call to worship, as many praise psalms do. The series of vows then serves as a description of *how* the speaker will worship: in this case, not with "harp and lyre" but with a "blameless life." In what ways are honesty and integrity acts of worship?

⊃ Almost all of this psalm consists of repeated pledges to associate with people of good character and not to associate with people of bad character. Is this the major factor that determines whether a person himself or herself will "lead a blameless life"?

3 As we saw in session 12, another important responsibility of ancient kings was to defend their countries against enemies by leading armies into battle. Psalm 110 promises Israel's king that God will fight for him, making sure that he has many strong, young, willing soldiers, and ultimately defeating the nation's enemies by his own divine power.

Psalm 110 is spoken to the king by a prophet or court musician. It's a prophetic oracle, an unusual form within the psalms. It first announces that it's being spoken on God's behalf: "The LORD says to my lord [the king] . . ." (A more common formula in the prophetic writings is, "Thus says the LORD.") The oracle then brings the message from God in poetic lines set to music. Have someone read Psalm 110 for the group.

While this psalm was probably composed at a time when the nation was threatened by enemy armies, and not necessarily on the occasion of a king's coronation, it does recall that occasion by reminding the king of the LORD's coronation oath to him: "You are a priest forever, in the order of Melchizedek." The name "Melchizedek" means "king of righteousness." It was probably an honorary title that the Jebusite kings of Jerusalem formerly held. When the Israelites conquered that city, their own kings assumed the title, along with the symbolic role of "priest," meaning that they were representatives of the people before God, but not that they offered sacrifices—this was reserved for the descendants of Aaron, Israel's actual priests. So the psalm envisions a righteous king defending his country against enemy aggression.

(Psalm 110 is also a Messianic psalm that the book of Hebrews in the New Testament uses to describe how Jesus is a representative before God of those who believe in him.)

⮞ Is your country's political leader also the commander of its armed forces? If not, how does this leader relate to those forces? What constraints are there on the authority to go to war and on what these forces can do when they are at war? When your country does go to war, how does this need to be justified?

FOR FURTHER READING AND DISCUSSION

Read and discuss these other psalms that depict the coronation of a king in Israel.

- Psalm 2 offers reassurance at a time when the nation is threatened by enemy armies. It recalls how God himself installed the king on the throne. This psalm refers to the king as God's "son" (just as Psalm 72 called him the "royal son"). This is another Messianic psalm. Jesus and his early followers used it to describe his special relationship with God.
- Psalm 21 similarly reassures the king of God's help in battle, recalling his coronation. (God "placed a crown of pure gold on his head.")
- Psalm 20 begins with a series of petitions for the king, like those in Psalm 72, and so it may also have been used at coronations.

FOR YOUR NEXT MEETING

In the next session you'll read through the Song of Songs, a short biblical book. Different people will be taking the parts of different characters: a bride, a groom, and the friends at their wedding. Prepare for this reading by having your group members pencil in the names of these characters in the margins of their copies of *The Books of the Bible*.* You can find these names ("she," "he," "friends") in standard editions of the NIV, including at biblegateway.com.

Everyone should at least mark the parts spoken by the "friends." Decide who will be taking the parts of the bride and groom and have them mark those parts as well. For these roles choose an actor and an actress, preferably a married couple, who are comfortable speaking the parts of these characters whose physical attributes and whose marriage and its consummation will be described in evocative imagery.

Alternatively, you can listen to a professional recording of the Song of Songs. The *NIV Audio Bible* by Zondervan is available through Christian bookstores and many online outlets. You may also search online for a free copy of the Song of Songs in audio format. However, in these recordings all the parts are read by the same speaker. For that reason, you may want to listen to the book using *The Bible Experience*, in which different actors read the separate parts. It's available in bookstores and online, including at the iTunes Store.

For background, group members may also wish to read the introduction to the Song of Songs in *The Books of the Bible* in advance of your next meeting.

---

* While the biblical text doesn't indicate specifically who's speaking at which points, this can be reasonably inferred from grammatical indications of gender and number in the original Hebrew. Many versions of the Bible add the names of the speakers to the text (NIV, ESV, NLT, etc.). These are not included in *The Books of the Bible* because one important goal of that edition is to distinguish the text itself from explanatory and interpretive material. However, to make it possible to read through the Song of Songs as a group, you can temporarily add these names in pencil. (You can also choose to read together out of another edition of the Bible that already has the names in it, but make sure that people don't use different translations, as there are slight discrepancies between them in the parts they assign to various speakers.)

PSALMS FOR SPECIAL OCCASIONS: MARRIAGE and THE SONG OF SONGS

INTRODUCTION

Weddings were another joyful special occasion that songs were written for in ancient Israel. One of the psalms, Psalm 45, was composed for a royal wedding between the king and a foreign princess. Another book of the Bible, the Song of Songs, is a collection of similar compositions that were traditionally sung at weddings in the land.

READING AND DISCUSSION

1 Have someone read Psalm 45 for the group. Note that the writer, probably a court musician, briefly praises the special character of this composition, addresses the king for eight lines, and then turns to address the "royal bride" for the final eight lines.

Like the psalms we considered in the last session, this one recalls the king's coronation and stresses his role in protecting the nation against its enemies and upholding justice within the land. (In this role he represents God, so the psalm actually addresses him as "God" at one point.) But on the occasion of this wedding, the singer also describes the splendor of the setting: the aroma of fragrant spices, the beautiful appointments of the palace, the music of stringed instruments. The psalm describes the king's royal robes and calls him the most "handsome" of men (NIV "excellent"; the Hebrew root is the same one used to describe the "beauty" of the princess). As the singer surveys the king and his surroundings, his eye comes to rest on the bride, and this provides an elegant transition into the final section.

The singer celebrates the new queen's gorgeous apparel, her attendants, and the rejoicing that surrounds her. But just as the psalm reminded the king of his responsibilities, it also speaks a word of admonition to the queen. She must leave behind her former life as a princess in another country and embrace her important role in this new court. (One likely translation for the third line addressed to her is, "Daughter of Tyre, with a gift the rich will seek your favor." This speaks of her new status and also of her need for discretion and integrity.) The psalm closes with a vision of this queen guiding the next generation of the royal house and winning a wide and lasting reputation.

⮑ Have you ever seen a royal wedding, either in person or on television? If so, tell the group what it was like and what you remember most about what you saw and heard.

⮑ If you've had a wedding of your own, what music did you choose for it? Why? If you're not married but think you might like to be, what music do you want to have at your wedding?

⮑ When the psalm tells the princess to "let the king be enthralled by your beauty," the most immediate reference is to her coming from a foreign land. The psalmist is urging her not to be downcast with mourning over the family and country she has left behind, but rather to be filled with a radiant, attractive joy as she embraces her new homeland and king ("lord"). But throughout the psalm, the handsomeness of the husband and the beauty of the wife are praised and celebrated alongside their qualities of character. How can men and women give the right amount of attention to staying in shape and looking their best, as something that's genuinely praiseworthy in itself, without becoming obsessed with a superficial cultural ideal of external beauty?

2 The Song of Songs is a book of the Bible that contains a collection of wedding songs from ancient Israel. It has a heading that attributes them to Solomon, the son of David who succeeded him as king of Israel. Since Solomon is known to have written many songs, he may indeed have been the original author of these. On the other hand, this heading could be like the ones in the psalms, which express a traditional understanding of authorship that we can't be entirely certain about. In that case, the songs could have been written by a variety of authors at different times, and the references they make to Solomon would reflect the custom, common in many cultures, of depicting a groom and bride as a "king" and "queen."

These songs have now been collected and arranged in such a way that they tell the story of a courtship and marriage and its consummation. The bride, the groom, and their friends speak in turn. (This may reflect the way that brides and grooms sang to one another, and their guests sang to them, at traditional wedding celebrations.)

Read through the Song of Songs as a group. This will take about 8 to 10 minutes. (You should have made the necessary preparations for this after your last meeting, as described at the end of the previous session.) Have the two people you chose read the parts of the bride and the groom, and have everyone else read the parts spoken by the "friends." Alternatively, you can listen to a recording of the book.

As you listen, you may not understand everything, since the Song of Songs uses extensive visual imagery drawn from an ancient agrarian setting. However, with a little reflection, you will be able to understand many of these images. For example, when the groom tells his bride, "Your teeth are like a flock of sheep just shorn, coming up from the washing. Each has its twin," he's complimenting her smile: her teeth are white, and none are missing! The book includes a brief dream sequence, introduced when the bride says, "I slept but my heart was awake." The book refers to the women of the city, particularly the bride's friends of marriageable age, as "daughters of Jerusalem." When it refers to men, particularly young men, it literally says "sons." This is why the groom sometimes refers to the bride as his "sister": they both belong to the family of Israel.

◌ Did you enjoy hearing the Song of Songs read aloud? What parts of the book were your favorites? Did you find any parts uncomfortable? If so, which ones and why?

◌ In your culture, or in a culture you're familiar with, are brides and grooms portrayed as queens and kings at their weddings? If so, how is this done?

◌ Like Psalm 45, the Song of Songs describes fine clothing, jewelry, and fragrances, and it depicts an opulent celebration with wine, delicacies, and music. Does the occasion of a wedding justify indulging in some luxuries like these? Why or why not? Does the appreciation expressed for these items here in the Bible mean that followers of Jesus can legitimately want to enjoy some of them from time to time? Is this consistent with accepting a responsibility to help the poor and live a simple life?

◌ The beauty of the bride is idealized in these songs. In several places her features are listed and praised, and she's described as "flawless" and "perfect." This reflects how the groom prizes her above all other women, and how this wedding day is her day to shine. The attractive features of the groom are similarly recounted, and he's described as "outstanding among ten thousand." Is there a danger that seeing language like this in the Bible could lead men and women into a costly, unhealthy, and even dangerous pursuit of an unattainable ideal of physical attractiveness?

◌ In many cultures today, particularly Western ones, sexual activity is often portrayed graphically and explicitly in movies, books, television programs, etc., even when these aren't intended to be pornographic. By contrast, the Song of Songs veils its depictions in symbolic language. Does a more indirect portrayal through evocative imagery preserve something of the mystery and beauty of human sexuality? Or should sexual activity be portrayed as realistically as possible in order for it to be understood and appreciated?

⮑ At three key points, two of them early in the book, the bride turns to her unmarried friends and says, "Daughters of Jerusalem, I charge you by the gazelles and by the does of the field [symbols of love]: Do not arouse or awaken love until it so desires." She's warning that while it's good for them to hear these songs so they'll appreciate the beauty of the human body and the delights of married love and sexual intimacy, they should also be careful not to arouse sexual desire until it can be honorably satisfied in marriage. Why is it the biblical standard that sexual relations should take place only within marriage? How can followers of Jesus today develop a healthy appreciation for sexuality but also practice self-control and treat others with honor and respect? What practical steps can people take to make sure they don't get too much information and stimulation from the media that surround them?

⮑ At the end of the book, the friends speak about a "little sister," a hypothetical young woman in their community, who needs to wait to get married because she's not yet physically mature, but who may nevertheless be "spoken for" and become engaged. They hope she will be a "wall" and keep the man out until marriage; if so, they will honor her. But if she would be a "door" and let the man in, they will have to keep the two of them apart. What safeguards can a dating or engaged couple put in place to make sure they don't spend too much time together in situations where they might be tempted to have sex before marriage? (The bride notes in this final song that she was a "wall," chaste until marriage, and that she's now physically mature, a delight to her husband.)

PSALMS FOR SPECIAL OCCASIONS: PILGRIMAGE

INTRODUCTION

All the people of Israel were commanded in the law of Moses to gather in Jerusalem three times a year for the great festivals of Passover, Pentecost, and Tabernacles, which celebrated their history and identity as a nation that God had chosen and blessed. These important and joyful occasions are mentioned in many of the psalms. For example, in Psalm 42–43, the psalmist longingly remembers going to "the house of God . . . with shouts of joy and praise among the festive throng." Some individual psalms were written specifically for and about the experience of going on a pilgrimage to Jerusalem for these festivals.

The book of Psalms also contains a group of short compositions, Psalms 121–134, that are called "songs of ascents." Most interpreters understand this title to mean that they were customarily sung by festival pilgrims on their way to Jerusalem. (The term "ascents" is used because going up to Jerusalem involved a climb of about three thousand feet, up Mount Zion.) These songs are written in a variety of forms, and while many of them refer directly to the journey and the festivals, they also speak about a broad range of other experiences.

In this session we'll first look at some pilgrimage psalms and then consider the songs of ascents.

⮑ What's the largest crowd you've ever been in that gathered for a special occasion? (For example, New Year's Eve in Times Square, the celebration of a national holiday in your capital, etc.) Tell the group what this experience was like.

⮑ What's the largest crowd you've ever been in that gathered specifically for a religious occasion? (A city-wide Easter service, a Christian music festival in a stadium or park, a papal visit, etc.) Tell the group about this experience. What would it be like if the people of your culture gathered for religious events in as great numbers as for the most important secular occasions?

READING AND DISCUSSION

1 Have someone read Psalm 84 for the group. In its form, this pilgrimage psalm most resembles a psalm of trust. It mostly describes the joy, contentment, and security of seeking and trusting God, with only a brief petition for the king towards the end ("Look with favor on your anointed one").

Psalm 84 remarks how blessed the priests and Levites must be who are always in God's house. But it says that those whose "hearts are set on pilgrimage" are just as blessed. This means devout Israelites who, like the psalmist, eagerly go to Jerusalem for the festivals. They experience God's goodness not only at the temple, but also on their way there. For example, they find springs of water in the Valley of Baka (probably an arid valley they need to pass through). They "go from strength to strength," sustained by similar blessings all along the way, "till each appears before God in Zion."

⮑ Have you ever gone on a pilgrimage, a journey to some significant religious site or in search of a deeper experience of God? If so, tell the group about it. Did you find that God was traveling along with you on this pilgrimage, surprising you with mercies along the way?

⮑ In session 7 you considered Psalm 139, another psalm of trust, and saw how a person of faith can be in God's presence anywhere in the world. The pilgrims described in Psalm 84 experience something of this themselves on their way to Jerusalem. But the writer still expresses a deep longing to be in the temple itself, the "dwelling place" of God. How do sanctuaries, spaces set apart for God, provide a unique experience of God's presence?

2 Psalm 24 also seems to have been written for the pilgrimage festivals, since it asks, "Who may ascend the mountain of the LORD? Who may stand in his holy place?" Some interpreters believe that a group actually sang these questions out to the crowds as they were coming up to the temple, and that the pilgrims affirmed the sincerity of their worship by responding with the next lines: "The one who has clean hands and a pure heart, who does not trust in an idol or swear by a false god."

Have someone read Psalm 24 out loud. Note that it begins by describing the LORD as the Creator and ends by depicting him, Israel's protector in battle, returning victoriously to the temple. The pilgrimage section is in between.

⮑ What would happen if someone stood outside the worship gathering of your community and challenged people to make sure they had "clean hands and a pure heart" if they were going to come inside?

⮑ Like Psalm 84, this psalm pronounces a blessing on those who come to God's temple in sincerity and devotion. Do you feel you've ever received a "blessing" by visiting a "holy place"? If so, tell the group about your experience. Do you think this happened because there was something special about the very ground you were standing on? Or did this visit become the occasion for this blessing in some other way?

3 Divide your group into four teams and have each one look at one of the following songs of ascents. Identify where and how each speaks to the experience of going on pilgrimage or of being in Jerusalem for one of the annual festivals. What type of psalm does it most resemble (psalm of trust, song of Zion, psalm of praise, etc.)? Do you see the themes of blessing, protection, or prayer that were in Psalms 84 and 24? What experiences of your own does the psalm call to mind? What questions does it raise for you? Do you know any songs or hymns that are based on it? Once all the teams have read and discussed their psalms, they should read them out loud for the group, share their insights, and pose their questions for everyone to consider.

- Psalm 121 ("The mountains" here probably refers to where Jerusalem is located.)
- Psalm 122
- Psalm 133 (This psalm uses two images to express a sense of refreshment: oil and dew. In this desert culture oil was poured on the head to rehydrate the skin.)
- Psalm 134

⮑ Conclude your time together, if you wish, by singing or listening to Brian Doerksen's song "I Lift My Eyes Up," which is based on Psalm 121.

FOR FURTHER READING AND DISCUSSION

- Read Psalm 15. How is it similar to and different from Psalm 24?
- As noted above, songs of ascents take a variety of forms and speak to a number of different situations. (You've already considered one of them, Psalm 131, in session 7 as a psalm of trust.) Read the following songs of ascents, and see how they're examples of the forms listed:
  - Supplication: Psalms 120, 123, 132
  - Thanksgiving: Psalm 124
  - Thanksgiving and supplication: Psalm 126
  - Trust: Psalms 125, 127

- Imprecatory: Psalm 129
- Penitential: Psalm 130
- Wisdom: Psalm 128

Why might pilgrims on their way up to Jerusalem have sung each of these psalms?

PSALMS FOR SPECIAL OCCASIONS: COVENANT RENEWAL

INTRODUCTION

Many interpreters believe there was one more special occasion in the life of ancient Israel that some of the psalms were written for: a regular (perhaps annual) ceremony of covenant renewal. Other interpreters dispute this idea, arguing that there's no actual proof a ceremony like this was held regularly at the temple. But the theme that the nation must make a renewed commitment to its covenant with the LORD does figure prominently in certain psalms that seem to be intended for use in a great assembly. In this session we'll consider several psalms that invite the people to gather and renew their covenant with the LORD, leaving open the question of whether these psalms were composed for an established regular celebration.

READING AND DISCUSSION

1 In Psalm 50, God calls for all of Israel to be gathered together in his presence so he can speak to them about keeping their covenant with him. Have someone read this psalm out loud.

Here God addresses two groups of people. The first are generally observing the covenant, but in a formal way, through the regularly prescribed sacrifices at the temple. God encourages them to pursue a more personal relationship with him by entering into the dynamic of supplication and thanksgiving you've been exploring throughout this guide. "Call on me in the day of trouble," God urges them. "I will deliver you, and you will honor me." In other words, put your faith on the line, watch me come through for you, and make this the subject of real praise and thanksgiving.

God also addresses the "wicked." They claim to be part of the covenant, but they're breaking its essential requirements. In language that alludes to the Ten Commandments, God describes how they're guilty of theft, adultery, and false witness. They actually believe these things are consistent with the character of God. He threatens them with destruction if they don't start living in a way that truly honors him as the "God of justice."

⊃ Which people in Psalm 50 do you identify with more? Why?
- Those who are going through the motions of religion, who need to put their faith on the line if they want it to become more real.
- Those who consider themselves religious or spiritual, but who don't see any connection between that and living for justice.

What steps do you need to take to respond to the challenge this psalm addresses to the people you identify with?

2 Have someone read Psalm 81 for the group.

This psalm was written for some ceremonial occasion in the life of the nation, since it begins with a call for the sounding of the ram's horn, as at the monthly New Moon celebrations and the annual pilgrimage festivals.

In its form and wording, Psalm 81 is much like Psalm 50. God speaks directly to the people and challenges them. There is a significant difference, however. In Psalm 81 the specific problem is not that the people are just going through the motions of worship or thinking they can do no wrong; they are actually worshipping and serving "foreign gods." The psalm issues a call for the people to return to their covenant God and so experience his protection and provision once again.

⮑ If you belong to a community of Jesus' followers, picture God gathering them all together and saying, as he does in Psalm 81, "Hear me, my people, and I will warn you." What does God say next?

3 Psalm 115 was also written for an occasion when the people of Israel gathered together, since it provides a vehicle for them to receive a blessing, as they did at the annual pilgrimage festivals. It doesn't depict the LORD calling on the people to answer charges. Instead, it boldly asserts that all the gods of the other nations aren't worth worshipping and serving, because they're lifeless idols. It therefore calls upon three groups of people to "trust in the LORD." These groups are "his people Israel" (literally "house of Israel," the people of the nation in general), the "house of Aaron" (the priests), and "those who fear the LORD," probably non-Israelites who have come to believe in the LORD and worship at his temple. Each group is given the opportunity to respond to this call and say, "I'm in!"—either for the first time or in a renewed way, by chanting the line, "He is their help and shield." The psalm then pronounces a blessing on each of these groups. It concludes with a call to offer, on the occasion of this gathering, the kind of worship God alone can receive from people living on earth.

Have one person read this psalm out loud. Divide everyone else into three groups, representing the ones listed above, and have them respond with "He is their help and shield" at the appropriate places.

⮑ What opportunities does your community give for people to say, "I'm in!" and openly pledge their loyalty to God for the first time? Are there also opportunities for people to renew their commitments? If so, how? If not, would you like to see your community offer this opportunity? If your study of the songs in the Bible has helped bring you to the place where you'd now like to say, "I'm in!" yourself, share this with your group. They can help you make this commitment publicly.

⮞ If you wish, conclude your time together by singing or listening to Chris Tomlin's song "Not to Us," which is based on the opening of Psalm 115.

FOR YOUR NEXT MEETING

In your final session you'll be experiencing the book of Psalms as a whole. You'll need to schedule a special meeting of at least three hours, plus time for breaks, to read through the entire book. It would be ideal to arrange to share a meal during or after the reading. If you're using this guide for a community Bible experience, your whole church should gather to do the session together. Ideally this should be done as a one-day retreat.

EXPERIENCING THE BOOK OF PSALMS AS A WHOLE

INTRODUCTION

In this final session you'll experience the book of Psalms as a whole by reading through it together. You'll appreciate and share the breadth and depth of the spiritual experiences expressed throughout the entire collection. This will be a celebration and culmination of your engagement with these ancient but timeless worship songs.

Now that you've learned how the forms of the various psalms enable them to communicate their distinctive messages, you'll engage each one with understanding and sympathy. When you hear a psalm begin, "Listen to my prayer, O God, do not ignore my plea," you'll recognize it as supplication. When you hear another one report, "In my distress I called to the Lord . . . from his temple he heard my voice," you'll know it's a psalm of thanksgiving. And so forth.

In addition, by hearing the whole book at once, you'll be able to follow the flow of the entire collection in the final shape it has been given by those who gathered the psalms together:

1. The first principle of organization is by authorship as it was traditionally understood. The book begins with a large collection of psalms attributed to

David that has a small group by the Sons of Korah in the middle. A short collection of psalms attributed to Asaph follows, then another by the Sons of Korah, and finally a long group of mostly anonymous psalms (which includes a dozen or so additional ones by David).

2. The entire collection is then divided into five "books." This is modeled on the way the Torah or law of Moses was divided into five books. It's a way of showing that the psalms can be read and studied as Scripture. The divisions correspond roughly to the authorship collections. David's psalms make up Books I and II; the division between them occurs where the first Korah group is inserted. Book III comprises the Asaph collection and the second Korah group. Books IV and V include the mostly anonymous psalms. A benediction, a statement blessing God, has been inserted at the end of each book. Each one says something like, "Praise be to the LORD, the God of Israel, from everlasting to everlasting. Amen and Amen."

3. Then, in a further shaping, individual psalms have been placed at the beginning or end of books so that the collection as a whole traces the outlines of Israel's national and religious history.

- Books I and II represent the monarchy period, before the exile, when Israel was ruled by its own king. Psalm 2, a coronation psalm, originally came at the start of Book I, to emphasize this monarchy theme. Book II ends with Psalm 72, another coronation psalm.
- Book III represents the exile. It originally began with Psalm 74, a lament over the destruction of Jerusalem. Book III ends with Psalm 89, a salvation history psalm that traces Israel's story up to the exile and ends with a petition for God to remember his "former great love."
- Book IV asserts that, despite the exile, Israel's true king Yahweh still rules over the world. This book includes several psalms that begin by declaring "the LORD reigns" (Psalms 93, 97, and 99). Book IV ends with Psalm 106, a salvation history psalm that concludes with a prayer for God to bring the people back from exile.

- Book V then represents the return from exile. It begins with Psalm 107, a psalm of thanksgiving for this deliverance. Book V, and the whole collection, ends with a resounding note of worship in a series of five praise psalms. One of these, Psalm 147, makes one more mention of the return from exile: "The Lord builds up Jerusalem; he gathers the exiles of Israel."

4. The final shaping of the book of Psalms took place when two wisdom psalms were placed in commanding locations, Psalm 1 at the beginning of the whole collection, and Psalm 73 at the start of Book III. The placement of these psalms signals that the experiences recorded throughout the book can be a source of wisdom to those who will meditate on them as they would the other Scriptures. This reinforces the message sent by the division of the whole collection into five books.

With this information about how the book of Psalms has been shaped, as you listen to it, you can relive the entire story of the community of Israel, even as you share the range of spiritual experiences its individual members have expressed.

READING

As a group or as an entire church, read through the book of Psalms together. Have people take turns reading one psalm each. (When you get to Psalm 119, have people read one alphabetical section each.) At the end of each of the five books the collection has been divided into, take a break for drinks and refreshments, and perhaps a physical activity if needed. Share a meal together at the end of Book III or Book V.

DISCUSSION

⮑ How would you sum up your experience with the book of Psalms over the past several months and in this complete reading? What will you remember most about the book? What things have you come to understand for the first time or in a new way? How has your relationship with God grown and developed?

⮑ Do you agree or disagree with the following statement? Why? "The psalms model for us a much broader and more honest expression of spiritual experience than we usually practice or allow in our own communities." If you agree with the statement, in what ways could your community encourage a more authentic expression of a wider range of feelings, questions, and experiences in relationship with God?

⮑ Have the psalms encouraged your own personal creative expression through music, poetry, art, or other media? If so, how?

⮑ Which is your favorite psalm? Why?

Clean. Beautiful. Unshackled.

- chapter and verse numbers removed
  (chapter and verse range given at bottom of page)
- natural literary breaks
- no additives: notes, cross-references,
  and section headings removed
- single-column setting
- whole books restored (Luke–Acts, Samuel–Kings, etc.)
- book order provides greater help in understanding

There is no Bible more suited to reading—from the beginning of the book to the end—than *The Books of the Bible*. This "new" approach is actually the original approach, and I love it.

Scot McKnight
North Park University

For more information or to download the gospel of John, visit www.Biblica.com/TheBooks. Watch this site for a four-volume set comprising the entire Bible in this format, coming soon.

ALSO AVAILABLE

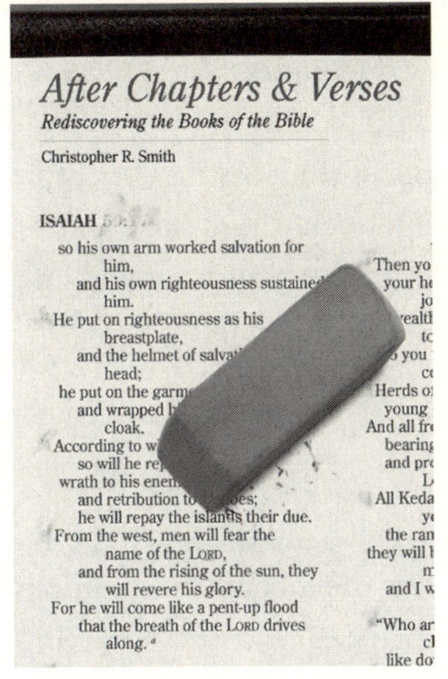

Bible reading is declining at such a rapid rate that within 30 years the Bible will be a "thing of the past" for most Christ-followers. One of the main reasons for this decline is the format of the Bible. The format we know today was created so that a "modern" world could divide and analyze and systematize the Scriptures. But this made the word of God practically unreadable. As we move into a postmodern world, we'll need to recapture the stories, songs, poems, letters, and dreams that naturally fill the pages of Scripture. Only then will a new generation of readers return to the Bible.

Christopher Smith argues in this book that the "time for chapters and verses is over." He explains how these divisions of the biblical text interfere with our reading and keep us from understanding the Scriptures. He describes how Biblica has created a new format for the Bible, without chapters and verses, with the biblical books presented in their natural forms. And he shares the exciting new approaches people are already taking to reading, studying, preaching, and teaching the Bible in this new presentation.

Paperback, 234 pages, 5.5 x 8.5
ISBN: 978-1-60657-044-9
Retail: $15.99

Available for purchase online or through your local bookstore.

ALSO AVAILABLE

There is an increasing recognition that we need to engage the Bible as a collection of books. But we haven't been taught to read or study the Bible on the book level. Almost all of our approaches to the Bible are based on chapters, verses, or sections, so how do we change this?

The units of meaning in the Bible are not chapters, or verses, or topical sections, but the literary compositions that God inspired to create the Scriptures. If we want to know the meaning of God's Word, we need to engage these compositions on their own terms. This means understanding why they were written, what kind of writing they are, how they are put together, and what major themes and ideas they develop and pursue. This book answers these questions for each of the books in the Bible by presenting expanded versions of the book introductions included in *The Books of the Bible*, an edition of the Scriptures from Biblica that presents the biblical books in their natural literary form, without chapters and verses.

Paperback, 176 pages, 5.5 x 8.5
ISBN: 978-1-60657-045-6
Retail: $15.99

Available for purchase online or through your local bookstore.